T0312071

Schematic Leadership Identity Model (SLIM)

A workbook for leaders who desire to be more effective and deliberate in their leadership identity and for young leaders coming into their own, this book introduces a unique two-step process to understand and define your leadership identity.

While some leadership frameworks operate under static concepts of what makes a good leader, the Schematic Leadership Identity Model (SLIM) offers new and seasoned leaders an opportunity to explore the anchoring of who they are and the ebbs and flows of their attitudes and behaviors through life's changes and experiences. The SLIM framework has two main footings of its seven phases: *revolution*, which is the recognition of one's identity journey, and the theoretical constructs that help frame the process and *evolution*, a series of assignments and journal entries that helps each leader acknowledge their current leadership identity, unravel habits and behaviors that may not align with their idealized self, and redefine their leadership identity based on their findings and whom they aspire to be. The evolutionary design is a system necessary to be revisited as a leader goes deeper into their memories and experiences. This framework helps unearth unconscious and implicit biases that can hinder a leader's social and cultural capital.

No matter the industry or discipline, SLIM offers leaders a self-guided process of discovery that can profoundly examine the root causes of behaviors and attitudes to create meaningful change within themselves that can produce significant positive changes in their teams and organizations.

Deatra L. Neal, Ph.D., was born and raised in Cincinnati, Ohio, and now resides in Atlanta, Georgia. She is an award-winning filmmaker who earned her Ph.D. in Global Leadership in 2021. Deatra has worked with many cultures and diverse perspectives as a global consultant, creative entrepreneur, professor, and researcher. Deatra seeks to foster a sense of identity in leaders, allowing them to mitigate biased behaviors and attitudes that support problematic outcomes for marginalized groups. Deatra's inspiration comes from her daughter, Jada, and grandson, Thomas, and her many great-nieces and great-nephews who will soon be in positions to change the world.

Schematic Leadership Identity Model (SLIM)

Utilizing History and Memory to Help Redefine Leadership Identity

Deatra L. Neal

Routledge
Taylor & Francis Group

NEW YORK AND LONDON

First published 2024
by Routledge
605 Third Avenue, New York, NY 10158

and by Routledge
4 Park Square, Milton Park, Abingdon, Oxon OX14 4RN

Routledge is an imprint of the Taylor & Francis Group, an informa business

Library of Congress Cataloging-in-Publication Data
A catalog record for this title has been requested

ISBN: 978-1-032-49490-6 (hbk)
ISBN: 978-1-032-49488-3 (pbk)
ISBN: 978-1-003-39405-1 (ebk)

DOI: 10.4324/9781003394051

Typeset in Times New Roman
by Taylor & Francis Books

Thank you, Lord, for Your constant grace, mercy, and love You give to me daily.

To my beautiful and talented daughter, Jada, for your never-failing inspiration, encouragement, love, and pure joy you bring to my life.

To my beloved grandson, Thomas. I pray that this work will help guide you on your leadership journey for I know that you will do incredible things in this world.

To my sisters, Deborah and Andréa, and my brothers, Warren, Michael, and André. Thank you for filling my life with love, laughter, and adventure. You all inspire me to be the best version of myself. I love you forever. To our angels – Marcus, Darryl, and Maurice – may you continue shining your light on us.

To my tribe of friends and family, those I speak to regularly, and those who still love and support me, no matter how much time has passed. A very special thank you to my sister Andrea Carter, my brother Michael Bell, Denise Simmons, Jeanette Vaughn, Ph.D., Monique Sneed, Sharon Williams, Pastor Deena Wingard, Naomi Duncan, and Damon Moats, who were there during those challenging periods in my life. Thank you for your council, mentorship, friendship, patience, and shoulder to cry on. May God continue to bless each of you.

To my angels in heaven, my parents, whose spirits continue to be with me daily – pushing me, guiding me, and reminding me that righteousness in the heart creates beauty in the soul.

To my ancestors for their perseverance through their unimaginable fight for freedom that birthed a culture so strong and undeniable that 400+ years of oppression and discrimination cannot contain it or break it.

Contents

Figures

Tables

About the Author

"I provide a framework to help leaders embrace their history and its importance in forming who they are today to build a model for the type of person and leader they want to be in the future."

Deatra L. Neal is a professor, researcher, and consultant with a Bachelor of Business Administration in Computer Information Systems, a master's degree in marketing, and a Ph.D. in Global Leadership and Change. In 2019 she received the Global Leadership and Change Provost Grant to further her research in a pedagogical framework that identifies creative ways to address social issues. Deatra has published several articles for *Le*

Figure 0.1 Deatra L. Neal, Ph.D.

Potentiel, the leading newspaper in Kinshasa, Democratic Republic of Congo, and she has published and presented at the Global Studies Conference in May 2021 and July 2023.

As an award-winning filmmaker, Deatra has written, directed, and produced several short films shown in festivals across the US and internationally and has taken home over 25 awards. She has worked alongside Nickelodeon writing executives and some of the most talented independent filmmakers in the industry. Her short film "What About Us?" was featured on the ASPIRE cable network and received the New York City Council's recognition for important community stories. Deatra co-produced the 2011 Sundance award-winning film *Kinyarwanda* and served as lead writer on several hour-long dramatic series for EbonyLifeTV, Africa's first Global Entertainment & Lifestyle network in Nigeria. Deatra seeks to construct a new organization that facilitates the unmasking and uncovering of the African diaspora's rich history and culture through creative storytelling and innovative technology.

As an unapologetic creative entrepreneur, Deatra uses art as a tool to educate and solve social issues. She believes her raison d'être – the reason for being – is to help cultivate a climate that encourages truth in one's identity, to inspire young minds to seek purpose and explore creative freedom "by any means necessary". She will continue to promote creative thinking to spark the innovation needed to elevate the human conditions in vulnerable regions to fuel financial growth and sustainability.

Deatra has a 23-year-old daughter, Jada, who has been a constant source of inspiration and motivation; and illustrated several images in this book. She has a 1-year-old grandson, Thomas Day Harris, lovingly called "Lil D" as a homage to her from her daughter, Jada. Deatra is the 7th of 9 children. She lost her parents 12 days apart in August 2018, the catalyst for her identity journey that fueled this research model.

Chapter 1

Introduction

Identity is a heavily researched topic across disciplines. In the social sciences, specifically psychology, identity is the sense of self. This perception is a derivative of all our experiences and memberships that inform and contribute to our behaviors, attitudes, values, and habits. In social psychology, social identity is the interplay between how we see ourselves independently and how we see ourselves within social groups. In philosophy, identity is more paradoxical in examining the mind processes versus the brain processes. Philosophers study identity in layers of sameness and difference. These varying definitions and approaches only scratch the surface of the complexities of understanding identity. Many people go through their entire lifetime and never really understand who they are. Some people attribute what they do to who they are, while others define themselves by their families or the company they keep. Roles and positions we ascribe – teacher, mother, friend, therapist, woman, friend, etc. – are prescriptive of how we see ourselves and society's identification of who we are.

All these offerings can be an essential part of identity, but this book and my research strive to understand the anchoring of identity. Identity goes much deeper than these surface characteristics. Is who we are merely a product of our environment? Is it something we can design on the fly? Is identity passed down through our DNA? Or is who we are closely aligned with our epistemological philosophy, meaning how we gain knowledge of self and depending on the sources? Many people are who they are by happenstance. Things happen in our lives that shift our focus and our direction. There is no way to prepare and plan for everything that will take place in our environments, workplaces, families, or social circles. If nothing else is certain, change is a guarantee. In many situations, change is good but good or bad, how can we designate how these changes affect who we are and how we show up in the world?

Some studies define identity with many things such as emotions and personality characteristics. Conflating identity with our feelings is easy, but these can change whenever the wind blows. Associating identity and the fluidity of emotions can be problematic. For most people, there is no

DOI: 10.4324/9781003394051-1

seismic altering of behavior, attitudes, and decisions that veer away from their core self. Those who exhibit rollercoaster behavior changes are often diagnosed with some social or psychological disorder. Psychologically, and at the core of identity theory is the search for authenticity in self. Schematic Leadership Identity Model (SLIM) provides a tool to help individuals find their identity foundation and build (or re-identify) who they aspire to be as leaders. We are all leaders, so this model can be helpful to everyone. The SLIM framework allows leaders to unpack and explore the perseverance of historical practices and normalized behaviors that inherently and unconsciously show up in attitudes, decisions, and behaviors. History and memories are the solidifying principles of SLIM. Their importance cannot be understated when evaluating yourself. Our history and memories are evidence that we exist and were here, and they provide a blueprint for clues that can help us navigate our future.

In this fast-paced world where everything is immediate and essentially at our fingertips, it can be challenging to make decisions "on the fly" that reflect who we are. Now more than ever, it is imperative that leaders pause to discern and dissect who they are and understand the impetus and grounding of their leadership identity to avoid decisions that are the antithesis of their core values and principles. It is important to balance personal values and beliefs with the ethos of an organization to allow leaders to meet the requirements of their roles and adhere to their obligations. This leverage requires leaders to understand their values and beliefs and set boundaries. Suppose one's core identity establishes when a person knows and fully understands their mission, vision, and value statements. In that case, it is easier for them to align the decision-making process for a job function in ways that meet personal expectations with integrity and consistency. A quick and unexpected change in identity is often a result of the lack of knowledge and understanding of the core of one's identity. SLIM is a tool that helps recognize and establish the core values, attitudes, ideologies, and behaviors that make up the essentials of identity.

As stated, the significance of knowing and understanding your history is instrumental in defining your identity. Historically, this knowledge has been weaponized and held hostage to prevent people from achieving their goals and objectives. One must ask oneself why? If history is irrelevant, why do so many people try to hide it, fabricate it, and deny its significance? History guides the future because it holds the lessons and experiences that established where we are today. The successes, the failures, the tragedies, and the good times are all captured in our past. So much of this book and the SLIM process focuses on our history because leaders can use it to analyze and design what they want for their lives moving forward, and who they are drives that outcome. Root cause analysis conducted on past events, personal experiences, and decisions can significantly indicate how to handle situations for better results. This process is also a measure of personal accountability.

For this reason, leaders can examine their personal history and memories to center their identity and foundational constructs of behaviors and attitudes. Understanding your family dynamics is essential to this process but is one of many historical examinations leaders should conduct. What you remember and how you have reacted to situations and circumstances are critical to carving out your identity framework. Did your behavior align with your family's expectations and values? What makes your behavior similar or different from what you remember about your parents, grandparents, and great-grandparents? Do the things that mattered to you then still matter now? Why or why not? Even cultural events from several previous generations matter in your identity journey, as will be discussed in greater detail in the coming chapters. Hopefully, many questions will be answered as you go through SLIM's journaling process. Journaling has been a significant factor in my own identity growth.

Through this process, I anchored my identity and developed a blueprint of how my experiences and histories influence my attitudes, behaviors, habits, and decisions, which frame my critical thinking. My identity shift coincided with the grief, loss, work, and relationship changes over the past five years. Repositioning my identity has been painful, but the journey created a beautiful experience that landed me in a peaceful place filled with gratitude.

I have always been a planner. I set goals and devise strategies on how to obtain those goals. But life always throws curve balls that can derail the roadmap to reach those plans. However, these roadblocks are central to building our identity schemas. I could not have imagined welcoming challenges and constraints as I do now and being grateful for the scars. I trust myself. I have proven that I can meet the most harrowing experiences while staying within the boundaries I established for myself. To get to this place, I had to let go of this imaginary person I wanted to be for everyone else, accept who I was then, and strategize on how to reach who I wanted to be in the future, which is my idealized and aspirational self. The truth was not pretty. But I trusted the process and was completely honest in acknowledging those habits and behaviors that needed to be changed, knowing that if I wanted to ascend my current self to become who I wished to be, I needed to define myself for myself (Audre Lorde)[1] and put in the work.

One's existential self is who we are through our actions (behaviors and habits). We must decide which attitudes, behaviors, values, and ideologies should be changed or removed from our identities, which is the cornerstone of the SLIM framework. I let go of destructive generational beliefs and practices that did not add value to my life. I let go of people who were toxic or constantly taking and not giving back because all of this affected my actions and ultimately hindered me from reaching my identity goals. And let me emphasize that identity goals are not static but very fluid and ever-changing. Yet, your identity foundation should anchor you despite tremendous life changes. Look at your identity work as a journey and not a destination.

As I recognize and accept experiences, memories, and histories leading to problematic decision-making practices and unwanted habits and behaviors, I give myself grace and forgiveness. I understand that forgiving myself is just as important as forgiving others. I accept that I cannot change the outcomes I have experienced. I can take responsibility for how I react to situations and use those outcomes as anchors to navigate decisions in the future. The journaling process was crucial in helping me unravel behaviors and visually see myself on paper. Recognizing and accepting what was and using it to craft and construct an identity that aligns with the mission, vision, and realities of the existential, idealized self are instrumental in guiding the necessary change.

As Patricia H. Hinchey stated in her book, *Becoming a Critical Educator: Defining a Classroom Identity, Designing a Critical Pedagogy,* "We act based on what we believe, and what we believe depends largely upon evidence drawn from our own life experiences." My goal in developing SLIM was to foster a sense of identity in people that will allow them to reacquaint themselves and unearth preconscious and unconscious memories that manifest in behaviors and attitudes. Regardless of the leadership role, each of us must create a framework for our identity that clarifies and supports our beliefs, values, and behaviors that align with our identity goals.

Who we are is reflected in everything we do and how we make decisions. It is important to set a framing around your identity model. Identifying unwanted behaviors and attitudes challenges the formation of other unwanted habits that lead to precarious and harmful choices and outcomes. Unconscious and implicit bias is not an excuse to perpetuate bad behavior; it should be a charge for getting to the root of the ideology that influences this behavior and thought process and inspires you to improve. As discussed in further detail in the book, your unconscious self is your existential self. When I think about the unconscious the words of the great Dr. Suess come to mind, "Today you are you! That is truer than true! There is no one alive who is Youer than You!" Think of your unconscious as "Youer than you" because it is. Those negative attitudes and behaviors that are being attributed to the unconscious are who you are deeply, so it's time to dig in and do the work to unravel and reidentify who you are.

SLIM's self-guided workbook gives leaders the privacy and structure to uncover those feelings and values to re-evaluate, redefine, and reposition themselves. This process will help clarify who you are but requires only work you can do. What comes out of this process will depend on the time, effort, and honesty you put into the exercises. Remember, change is a process. Give yourself grace. Be gentle and understanding of your memories and experiences. Recognize that even the most challenging things we have gone through give us a deeper perspective of who we are. Utilize your history to guide your future self. We need you to show up as you – entirely and unapologetically!

SLIM's identity framing process resembles a DIY house construction or renovation process, with the house representing your identity. There are layers to your identity, like levels to a multi-story home. If you are from the Midwest like I am, you are familiar with the underground basements that are often dark and damp. If the levels of our identity were aligned with the levels of some multi-level homes, the main living areas would be equivalent to our consciousness. Most people dwell in this area frequently and are most comfortable. The attic space would represent the pre-conscious. This smaller square footage area, rarely used or visited, stores things for easy access. The preconscious is the area of the mind where short-term, repressed memories, behaviors, and attitudes reside and, with little effort, could be easily retrieved and accessed. The basement, often a dark, damp, and for some, the scary section of the home, is equivalent to our unconscious. It is the closest to our foundation. Even though it's part of the home, some homeowners prefer to avoid going into these underground basements that often have concrete walls. These rigid walls represent the blockages in our memories that make it difficult to recall and retrieve memories of our past.

SLIM's process is the tool to help chip away at the cement walls of your unconscious and unlock those memories that are key to understanding and acknowledging how certain behaviors, values, and attitudes developed. In many movies, a basement is a scary place. Similarly, the unconscious is a presumably uninviting place that many refuse to explore. It is crucial to understand the bare bones of your identity, without the décor crafted for the outside world, whether it is a professional role, a personal relationship, or an identity, one believes one should have. Discovering self requires spending time in all levels of your identity construction: the attic (preconscious), the main level (conscious), and the basement (unconscious).

Those who have built homes understand the stress, labor, and time it takes to complete this project. Your identity journey is similarly taxing. A leadership identity blueprint is essential to understand the aspirational self – whom you aspire to "be." Far too many do not work to recognize and acknowledge the foundation and build the framework around who they are; they jump right into the design phase of making themselves outwardly pretty, acceptable, and likable. If you have ever worked with contractors, you know that sometimes you cannot get the house designed as planned and hoped. In certain situations, you must let those things that are not safe, economical, or practical go. These adjustments to the identity blueprint may include releasing certain people who were initially part of the plan. Also, like building a home, sometimes an "add-on" may be restrictive. Re-constructing your identity may require some agility and

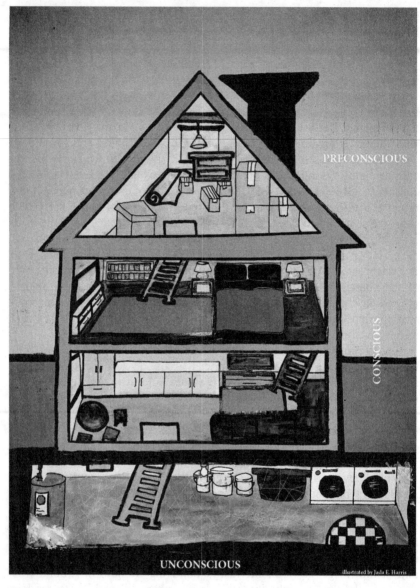

Figure 1.1 Levels of Human Consciousness

recognizing those limitations, such as releasing some expectations of how you see yourself that are not attainable or removing those things that may not lend themselves to reaching your authentic self.

Your identity journey is something that you must do alone. The catalyst to inspire you to go through this journey is that you want to be a better version of yourself. This book will waste your time if you do not want to be a better person and leader. Wanting to be a better human being is a daily endeavor that requires considerable thought, planning, and implementation until it doesn't. Progress in this arena is often a matter of finding good ground to build on, tearing down walls, shifting your framing and mindset, building, and designing, only to have to begin again after a few years or when a life-changing experience hits. My best advice as you go through this process is to – **spend some time in the basement!** The basement (the unconscious mind) is where you will find those things essential to who you are now, which may be holding you back from achieving your idealized self and restricting you from reaching your purpose. Or you may find that jewel you were reluctant to bring to the surface and put on full display. After reading this book and going through the SLIM process, you will have the tools and knowledge to strengthen your leadership identity and walk in the fullness of your aspirational self. You will be situated to be the lead architect of your newly structured, redesigned, remodeled, or reconstructed identity.

Cheers to your revolutionary identity journey!

Chapter 2

My Identity Journey

Identity is a novel concept that fascinates me. So many elements make up who we are physically, physiologically, psychologically, socially, and environmentally. Everyday experiences alter who we are in some way. Some changes are barely noticeable, while others bring about stark contrasts. People we meet, places we go, things we do, and things we hear and see can have long-lasting effects on our attitudes, behaviors, values, and beliefs. So, when do we settle into our identity if this is the case? How do we know who we are and what is artificial or the stuff (characteristics, behaviors, and attitudes) of convenience?

Journaling and examining my memories (family history, societal history, and generational and transgenerational history) answered many questions regarding my past, and memories inform my decision-making today. I would be remiss if I did not mention that I am still on my journey. I recognize this is a lifelong process, and I am open and committed to being vulnerable and honest with myself through the transitions. So, part of that vulnerability is sharing my story and explaining how this model continues to help me become a better person and, ultimately, a more effective leader.

I didn't realize I had been on my identity journey most of my life until I began my deep dive into researching identity. When I was in the 5th grade, I found my original birth certificate. Reading the information in this document would be central to questioning my identity. I will come back to this during my summary of my identity journey. As I go through my recollection, I will identify those behaviors, attitudes, and habits I added to my Schematic Identity Model Framework, revealed through the reflective journaling process and assignments along this identity journey.

Early Memories

My Childhood

I grew up in Cincinnati, Ohio, the seventh of nine children. My eight siblings (from oldest to youngest): Deborah, Warren, Marcus, Michael, Darryl,

DOI: 10.4324/9781003394051-2

Maurice, Andrea, Andre, and I grew up in a tightly knit family. My youngest siblings, Andrea and Andre, are twins. Three of my brothers – Maurice, Marcus, and Darryl – are now deceased. Due to our age differences, I have few memories of living with my three older siblings because they were already out of the house when I was a toddler. My third oldest brother, Michael, left the house after high school but was always there to hang out with us and help my parents whenever possible. He and I have always been close, and he played an important role in one of my most significant memories. So, that left five of us in the home for most of my upbringing. We lived in a quaint three-bedroom home. My parents were crafty and constantly took on projects around the house. They finished our basement and built a bedroom, laundry room, and a larger area used as an entertainment space for their parties and for us to play with our neighborhood friends. Our basement – nicknamed "The Cave" – when empty seemed large and frightening when I was young. But, when my parents had parties or our friends were over, "The Cave" was filled with joy, love, and good times.

We lived in a community called Skyline Acres. Skyline is on the west side of Cincinnati, a predominantly Black middle-class neighborhood. The families were close and accountable to each other. If you needed something, you could seek a neighbor to help. Growing up, I was deemed a bashful kid in school because I was quiet. During my identity journey, I realized that this was a label that others assigned to me, not one that represented who I was. I was skinny and tall, and I spoke with a lisp due to my tied tongue until middle school. My brother Marcus would tease me relentlessly and mock how I communicated. He was hilarious and could have easily made a living as a comedian.

Somehow, I did not take his jokes personally. Probably because he would show me so much love to offset the teasing; although I was quiet, he would remind the family how strong-willed I was at home and around friends. He would tell the story of when one of my neighborhood friends would come over. She would always want things her way. She tried to pick the games we played and always wanted to go first. He recalled that one day, I did not appreciate her selfishness, and when I refused to go along with her plans, she threatened to go home and never return. Imitating my lisp, he would share my sassy response: "Okay, go home then." This memory is interesting because I recall being unphased by things, including kids not liking me or picking on me for various reasons. Although people constantly filled our house, I genuinely enjoyed being alone or sitting in a room full of people, just listening and watching the interactions. People would label me bashful (or shy), but I never felt that way. I was never timid or afraid to speak; I did not want to talk, especially in class. Now, after doing the work, I realized I would refrain from speaking when I did not feel valued or seen in places, or when I simply wanted to take in the environment.

Being around my family in our home and living in the Skyline Acres neighborhood were places where I felt seen and valued, and it made for a beautiful way to grow up. My family and Skyline Acres were my first introductions to what a community should be and being "my brother's keeper." My childhood experiences, neighborhood, and family are important factors in who I am today. I believe in community and accountability to your family, friends, and neighbors to establish loyalty, a key characteristic of my identity. I realized that loyalty could be a double-edged sword if not utilized with discretion by framing your boundaries and understanding what and who serves your growth and well-being.

MEMORY ENTRY:

1   Loyalty and a sense of being a part of a community (value)
2   Being alone (behavior)
3   Stubbornness (behavior)

Reflecting, I believe that my silence and solitude were a way for me to protest being in environments that did not serve me well (school), or it was a way for me to take in information (home). Even though our neighborhood was predominately Black, the district bused many of us to a predominately white school. I did well in school and found myself in advanced placement classes, often the only Black student or with my dear friend, Darryl, from the neighborhood. Being quiet allowed me to observe people and conversations. I did not trust many of my teachers as early as elementary school. My memories of my school years include incidents of being disrespected. I can't recall entire situations, but I remember moments like being pinched by a teacher and having teachers laugh at my hair on picture day and administrators being shocked that my mother was so present at school. I vividly remember a parent–teacher conference with my sixth-grade teacher. She told my mother I needed to be in advanced classes away from my friends because I was different from those I hung around with in school. I did not receive this as a compliment but instead as offensive. Some may argue that this could have been the teacher trying to express my academic potential. Still, as a Black person, it is difficult to explain to non-Black people how racist and discriminatory comments and actions build up over time. Today, scholars have named these remarks and behaviors implicit bias and unconscious bias, but that does not remove the residual outcome of the effects on those impacted by them. The nuance of these comments over time, for decades, has had a lasting impact on my ability to trust, especially some white people.

However horrible this may seem; it is the truth, and this journey is about being honest with yourself and staying true to your memories and experiences. This admission was challenging to acknowledge, but the truth has allowed me to grow and use discernment instead of pre-judgment. I still exhibit these attitudes and behaviors of quiet observation, trepidation, and mistrust in some social environments.

Throughout my lifetime, I have had horrible experiences with racism, and I cannot wipe that out of my memory or rewrite my experiences to spare feelings or to fit into a normalized perspective of being "politically correct." Because I learned to be honest about my past, this has allowed me to be more amenable to building solid relationships, even with some white people who are open and willing to be forthcoming in discussions about race and racism.

Growing up in a large family can challenge children to unravel their identities. I recognized early in life that what was important to me may not be necessary to my brothers and sisters, and that is okay. In some families, kids grow up with similar personalities and passions. In my family, we were all very different, even my younger twin siblings. Looking back, I realize that our parents raised us to be independent and treated us as children with distinct personalities, interests, and idiosyncrasies. My parents recognized this and that each child had different challenges growing up. I had to contend with relentless teasing, not solely from my brother. Being teased for being tall, skinny, and dark-skinned were challenges I faced in elementary and early middle school. I refused to allow people to see my feelings hurt, so I pretended that what they said did not matter. If I ignored it, they would get tired and move on to the next kid, which is what happened. But I felt a lot of resentment and hurt, ultimately affecting my ability to trust people, including my friends. I became more adamant about my opposition to being teased and bullied in middle school. I was head and shoulders taller than most kids by then, and I used it to my advantage. The problem I found with keeping things in and not expressing how things bothered me at that moment resulted in significant blow-ups. Insulating my feelings was a habit that I recognized, acknowledged, and included in my SLIM model as something that I wanted to change.

MEMORY ENTRY:

1   Pre-judgment and distrust of white people who exhibit discriminatory behaviors, attitudes, and habits (behavior)
2   Cautious of establishing friendships (behavior)

My Mother

Figure 2.3 Mom at home, 1973As I started my identity journey and began to tap into my memories and history, my earliest memory is one of me and my mother. I was two, maybe three years old. I was in the kitchen, standing on a chair next to the kitchen table, watching my mother make a cake or cornbread. She gave me the spoon afterward to lick. This memory may seem frivolous, but as I began going through my

Figure 2.1 My Momma, Dolores E. Neal

process, this memory had significant meaning in my identity. This memory has been with me for decades. Still, as I searched for the importance of my experiences and how they could contribute to who I am, this recollection was central to understanding certain behaviors and attitudes. Once I began to dissect this memory, it became clear that my mother made time for me. If I was two or three years old in this memory, my siblings ranged from newborns to late teenagers. Considering how many people were in the house, it was striking that only me and my mother were in this memory. And this was not my only memory of moments spent alone with my mother. But even more precious were the memories when our entire family was together. I am sure some of my mother's happiest moments were when we were all together, laughing, eating, and playing games. Our backyard was large, lined with trees including pine trees and two beautiful plum trees. We had volleyball nets, swings, and room to have relay races. My mother loved to cook out and have my siblings and their families over. My mother had her flaws and idiosyncrasies, certainly, but she was special. Her sternness could be construed as mean or not easy to get along with, but once you got to know her, she was one of the sweetest people you would ever want to meet who would give her last to those she loved.

Family

I respected her greatly because she respected me, even as a child. Giving me respect should not be confused with a carte blanche on my behavior. She ran a strict household and enforced the delineation between being a child and an adult. Generations of Black adults raised their children on the premise that a child needs to stay in a child's place. Culturally and historically, for Black adults, this meant that children should not participate in or be in the presence of adult conversation and adult business. Younger generations of Black parents have seemingly loosened this culturally, possibly because of the ease of access to adult content and information children have on their phones and electronic devices via the Internet. Nevertheless, my parents, particularly my mother, had subscribed to this principle.

Not all my siblings had the same memories of my mother. It was not until after my parents passed that I realized my siblings and I had varying experiences with my mother. We could have the same memories, but their perspectives could differ from mine. They revered and respected her as our mother, which attributed to how she raised us. Even though their reasoning may have been different, the outcome was consistent with mine. Even if you grow up in the same house and do the same things it does not mean the perspective and one's "truth" is the same. Truth vs. perspective was another critical attribute I spent time meditating on and analyzing.

I realized that I would often set expectations for everyone, which was the source of most tension I had with my siblings. How I loved my mother was how I wanted them to love her. What I did for my mother, I wanted them also to do. The things that I did to care for my mother were the things I thought they should do to care for her. It was not until I stood outside my mother's hospice room after she died that reality hit me. Who was I to tell them how to love my mother or what they should do for my mother? This idea of setting expectations of others was a waste of my time and energy and something that I had to stop for my sanity. I am still trying not to put expectations on people. Sounds easy enough, but this is a daily, moment-by-moment conscious practice. Revisiting this time was therapeutic, cathartic, and significant for my identity journey.

MEMORY ENTRY:

1   My mother's love and friendship (value)
2   My childhood experiences at home remind me that everyone is different, it does not matter if they belong to the same group (racially, socially, family, or professionally), each person offers different perspectives and experiences that can enlighten and educate (value). Everyone can have different "truths" about the same memory.
3   Stop setting expectations for people and judging them by how I would like them to behave (behavior)

Looking back on my childhood, I appreciate how my parents raised my siblings and me. My mother was busy running a convenience store, selling Mary Kay, being a wife and mother, and entertaining friends and family in our home often, yet she found time to spend memorable moments with our family. Indeed, my siblings surely felt the same way at some point growing up, but I do not have the answer. At some point in our lives, we all felt as if we were our mother's favorite. Mom's favorite was a running joke between us, and before my mother's passing, I wanted her to confirm that I was indeed her favorite. When I leaned over in her bed and kissed her cheek, I whispered, "There is a kiss from your favorite." She looked at me and said adamantly, "I don't have a favorite." I chuckled, but on the inside, I wanted to cry. But then I smiled, realizing just how special she was. I tried to keep this conversation between us my little secret and torture my siblings about me being her favorite. Still, I happily shared this revelation with them because, as my siblings suggest, I cannot hold water.

Finding moments for nine children must have been difficult for my mother to accomplish. My mother mothered us with a firm hand. She believed in discipline – not physical punishment, but almost military-like discipline in how we should do things and treat people. Order was necessary to keep her home as she liked it and raise children who would grow up independent and self-sufficient. But she did not spare the rod if the situation warranted. Back then, if OCD were a thing, she would have most likely been diagnosed. Even though kids filled our house, our home was always immaculate, and I mean baseboards, walls, window seals, and anything that gathered or collected dust. Our friends knew if they came over on Saturday morning, she would put them to work and feed them well.

As I found out doing this work, how parents raised children and how mothers (mostly) kept the home is an inter- and transgenerational behavioral trait in our bloodline. My mother's behavior was much like that of my grandmother, great-grandmother, and great-great-grandmother. They all supported our immediate and extended families. Historically, in Black culture, the role of the mother is equivalent to strengthening and preserving the family and extending that to the community. During slavery, enslaved Black mothers fed children, who they did not give birth to, from their bosoms while their biological children, snatched from their arms, were sold into slavery. Black mothers had to be inventive, creative, and caring. They had to be firm and strategic with how they raised their offspring and, in many situations, the offspring of others. Black mothers represent the community because they are the originators, the foundation, and the glue that holds it together. The inter- and transgenerational family dynamics that I experienced are because of the Black women in our family.

My mother had three siblings, one brother, two sisters, and hundreds of first cousins. My mother, grandmother, and great-grandmother raised us as a unit, a community. We had huge family gatherings that most would consider annual family reunions, but we had them often throughout the year. We were always together as a family and a unit. Ingrained in the fiber of who I am is this sense of community. I am my brothers', sisters', cousins', family, and friends' keeper.

MEMORY ENTRY:

1   Order and cleanliness. For leadership, this equates to how I strategize and plan (habits)
2   Unlock inter- and transgenerational traditions and habits – Community is essential (value), a participatory family, being engaged and showing up for one another (value)

My Dad and My Father

As stated at the beginning of this section, one significant memory that changed my identity framing was finding my original birth certificate. When I was around eight years old, I found my birth certificate that indicated the man I thought was my daddy was not, and my birthday was a day different from the day I had been celebrating. The man named on my birth certificate was my mother's first husband, the father of my six older siblings. Ironically, not many people knew that we had different fathers because we never identified ourselves as half-siblings or stepsiblings. My mother's first husband, Willie Bell, was a retired Harlem Globetrotter. He had the financial means to care for my mother and older siblings but chose not to be responsible. The man that raised me, Edward Neal, married my mother, who had six children. They married when I was two years old. The twins were born the year they married.

When I asked my mother about the birth certificate, she told me she was still legally married to her first husband, which is why he had to be on the birth certificate. She and my dad went to the court to officially have my name and birth certificate changed in 1979 when I was 12. But this did not stop my inquisition. When I asked my mother again about my birth certificate from high school, she diverted and began telling me about her labor with me. The doctors had to use forceps to turn me into the womb. She stated that my near-breached birth was her most challenging. She noted that her labor with me was even more difficult than her experience with the hospital, leaving the afterbirth inside her womb and sending her home after the birth of my younger twin siblings. Her deflection only caused me to question who I was regarding my biological father.

Seeing this document had me questioning who I was throughout my teenage years. Nevertheless, I grew up with a loving dad. Edward Neal was one of the most gentle, caring, and nurturing men I have ever known. He loved my mother with every fiber in his body and often expressed it to her and anyone else who would listen. My siblings and I were blessed to have him in our lives. On August 16, 2018, my siblings and I stood around our dad's bed as he transitioned. Watching him take his last breath was highly emotional for all of us. I was angry and hurt because my daddy had pneumonia, and his transition was painful. For all my life, I remember him being a kind, sweet, and loving man, and to see him leave this world in pain was one of the most awful things to witness and to unravel.

Edward Neal ~ Daddy

Twelve days later, on August 28, 2018, my mother, Dolores Elizabeth Neal, transitioned. My parents shared a room in the hospice, and from the day my dad passed, my mother slept until she took her last breath. They were married for 53 years. My parents were very close, and since I can remember, they were always together. Their identities were connected and anchored, so much so that we worried about how one would survive without the other. We received the answer in August 2018, the worst month I had experienced in my entire life.

Included in that tumultuous month was the death of my 19-year-old great-nephew, found hanging in a tree at a lake where he would often go fishing. Three months later, one of my older brothers would unexpectedly die due to complications from a procedure he was undergoing. The grief my family experienced during the last two quarters of that year was insurmountable.

In 2019, a year after the death of my parents, I found out through an ancestry DNA test that Willie Bell was indeed my biological father. It took me a moment before I could process what I was seeing. It was an answer I had wanted for so long, but, ironically, when I received it, the result did not change much of what I felt about my mother or my dad, the man who raised me. We all were so blessed to have Edward Neal in our lives and his loving spirit has impacted who I am and certainly how I love.

Daddy and Me

I realized then that I have been on my revolutionary identity journey practically all my life. I have been questioning who I was since I was eight when I found my original birth certificate. As a child, uncovering that my last name was Bell, not Neal, and that the man listed as my father was not the man I called daddy was devastating. But I handled

Figure 2.2 My Daddy, Edward Neal

it like I handled the bullying – I pushed it deep down so that no one would know it affected me. I am grateful to God that I did not allow that to hinder me from loving my dad wholeheartedly. There are nuances in my identity that I am still unraveling, but I appreciate more who I am as I continue this journey. I could have handled the concern of my birth certificate in so many ways, yet I am proud of how I processed this information due to my love, respect, and reverence for my mother. I realize she gave me the best gift she could have ever given me. She allowed me to experience a dad. I have no pictures of Willie Bell. I have a few memories of meeting him and our conversations, mainly around my basketball career. I know he abandoned my mother and my siblings, and I witnessed the hurt they endured. He asked them for forgiveness before he passed. My prayer for my siblings is that they have received what they need to move on without malice in their hearts, and I hope there was a resolution with whatever he needed within himself.

Utilizing my history and memory has helped me understand many things about my actions and behaviors. Knowing that I was almost breached (coming into the world feet first instead of entering with my head!) at birth aligns with how I approached things in my life. During my identity journey, I utilized how I almost joined the world in understanding my behavioral patterns, especially in my teens and 20s, which resulted in my quick responses (diving in feet first) without fully thinking them out.

Reflecting on these memories and acknowledging the truth in my experiences helped frame the source of some of my behaviors and attitudes today. Even though I am much more outspoken and confident, I am still quiet in some circumstances. Still, I'm not too fond of ultimatums or feeling like someone is trying to control me. As far as I can remember, I have always had an issue with being disrespected. I realized my parents had a significant role in my aversion to disrespect. This disinclination may stem from my trying to hold on to some sense of self since this early age.

MEMORY ENTRY:

1   Like almost coming into the world "feet-first" (breech), I was used to making quick, hasty decisions before I learned to pause and consider (behavior)
2   Keeping my feelings to myself (behavior)
3   Don't like ultimatums, or feeling as if I'm trying to be controlled (value)

At some of the darkest times in my life, I seek ways to understand myself and uncover why, where, and how certain behaviors and attitudes became a part of my leadership identity. Bruce Lee once stated that what you are not changing, you are choosing. So, suppose you recognize things about yourself – habits and behaviors that do not align with your aspirational self or who you want to become. In that case, you are doing yourself a disservice and could be hindering yourself from reaching your personal goals.

I know now that my memories and histories influence my values, attitude, behaviors, habits, and decisions. What I experience in life shifts, molds, and strengthens my identity. Giving myself grace has come at a hefty price – years of trying to tip-toe around everyone else and concealing myself. Reflecting on the best and worst times in my life, I realized that's when the seismic shifts occurred in my identity. In 2018 after the loss of my parents, grief showed me another layer of myself, but it did not come without a lot of pain and tears. This process began with the realization that I no longer had my best friend, my confidante – my mother to help me when I hit those bumps in the road or to help me celebrate my wins. I did not have my daddy, one of the most loving and generous people I have ever known. He was always the provider, the nurturer, the calm in the storm, the "hugger," and the one who developed the blueprint for how I wanted to be treated by a man. What was I going to do? How would I navigate through this harsh life without the people who have been anchors for over 50 years? God provided me with the answer. He reminded me that He was always here with me and would give me what I needed. And He has done just that, which required work from me. As I continue this journey, I bravely explore my history and memories, hoping to always land in a place of peace and gratitude.

Between 2018 and 2019, I began my doctoral program just as I experienced the deaths in my family. During the program's first semester, I opened myself up to collaboration, only to have my IP stolen. As a creative thinker, everything I create is a part of me, and having it taken (stolen) is a loss. Because of who I am, I did everything possible to receive justice and restoration for this wrongdoing. Like many seeking justice in broken systems in this country, I did not receive it – not how I initially wanted it. At this time, another loss of anything would have taken me out. I had to recalibrate and be still to find the lesson in all these losses. I took a slow dive into depression in 2018 and did not realize it until 2021 while writing my dissertation. Depression shows up differently for everyone. My depression showed up as isolation. Ironically, it was during the global pandemic, so it may not have been visible to others. I am grateful to God that I was living with my younger sister at this time. We had each other to lean on and allowed each other the space to grieve and untangle what we needed to move forward.

This process of dealing with depression helped me strengthen my leadership identity because it resulted in me spending a significant amount of time alone, working through grief, and trying to find myself in this life, precisely without my parents. This period of loss has taught me not to try to control outcomes. Things that are out of my control happen in life, and I must guard my emotional health, which led to a deep scaling into my history and memories. These family memories reveal contractions in my behavior and leave me with so many more questions about myself. Who I am is what time, history, and circumstance have made me, but so much more (James Baldwin). These complexities are what make us unique if we can embrace them.

Five years later, I am still processing the losses I suffered, especially the loss of my parents. I have learned that loss opens space. Gaining space is not meaning to replace but to expand. I do not believe I would have been able to tackle some of my memories and spend time reflecting so intensely had I not lost my parents. Of course, I would rather have them here, but understanding the life cycle has made it easier and allowed me to be amenable to living fully and embracing life's experiences.

These are just snippets of my identity journey. A historical analysis of memories helped build out my identity schema for my SLIM framework. Later in Chapter 10, you will see how these memories helped me re-identify who I am as a leader and build my leadership identity schema.

Chapter 3

Phase I

The Revolution – The Foundation

The Planning Process

Poet and musician Gil Scott-Heron's (1971) popular song, "The Revolution Will Not Be Televised", described how the fundamental changes that matter come from an active, participatory position – an internal, reflective process. Reflection is the foundation of self-identification. The process is rooted in epistemology – understanding one's belief about self from the opinions of others subscribed to for self.

As we age, our identity tends to settle. Just like an older house, cracks begin to show when it settles more and more. For this journey, consider identity as a construction project. Building a home or any structure, you know that there must be preparations to secure a strong foundation. Utilizing a blueprint or outline to define the framing of the structure is helpful to keep things on track. These are similar processes outlined in SLIM to re-identify your leadership identity. Let's look at how the foundational essentials for building a house mirror the foundational necessities for (re) establishing one's identity. The ground carries the most significant responsibility in any construction project. According to many engineers and construction experts,[1] a solid foundation requires:

1 Construction that sustains imposed loads and pressures that may impair stability,
2 A rigid base for unbalanced settlements that are not evenly distributed,
3 Deep establishment to guard against swelling or shrinkage of the top layers.

Construction that sustains imposed loads and pressures that may impair stability

Think about how often in life the pressure of a situation causes a shift in our essential self. The transition is sometimes temporary, but too often, the

DOI: 10.4324/9781003394051-3

behavior or attitude change is permanent due to needing to craft an outcome or align with expectations of your role or the imposition of others who may see the role in a particular way. A strong foundation will secure heavy loads and support destructive and unexpected incidents. Like land surveyors, leaders must spend time surveying their identity boundaries and identifying unique behaviors, attitudes, and values features. This process will garner tools to help build and establish your leadership identity schema that outlines the specifics of who you are. SLIM utilizes historical memories and indicators to develop the core of one's identity by which a leader can formulate who they are currently and map a pathway to who they aspire to be.

A rigid base for unbalanced settlements that are not evenly distributed

A firm core identity foundation is an identity that is established and unshakable under challenging times. Of course, at times, leaders need to adjust and be amenable in situations to meet the goals and objectives within their jobs, but this can be done without infringing on their personal values and goals. Having a rigid core does not mean being inflexible in one's thought process or going against an organization's ethos. It does mean acknowledging one's ethos and balancing that in a way that meets your organizational role's responsibilities. Sometimes leaders must resolve several problems at once. When this happens, some may easily decide based on what others want or expect. This need to be swift could lead to decisions that are the antithesis of one's core character. There are ways to make decisions that meet your organization's needed outcomes and align with your values. When leaders have a footing in their identity and have established frameworks from which they work, their decisions will better align with their core values, beliefs, and behaviors indicative of their idealized selves. SLIM gives leaders a framework to build upon and adjust as necessary while holding onto those fundamental characteristics that make them who they are.

Deep establishment to guard against swelling or shrinkage of the top layers

There are definite layers to identity. Understanding identity as a foundation can help guard against the top layer or the artificial layer of the psyche from becoming dominant in actions and behaviors. Later in this book, the mind's preconscious, conscious, and unconscious layers will be evaluated and examined as central to one's leadership identity.

The strength of a house lies in its foundation. A well-designed foundation supports the load of the entire structure. History serves as the foundation for who we are. Knowing the details of our past is vital to help prevent cracks in the foundations of our identity. The lack of knowledge or the refusal to acknowledge your history can weaken us and holds us back from becoming our idealized selves. Ignoring our history and denying our generational traits, values, and beliefs creates a false sense of self and weakens the structural anchoring that frames who we want to "be." Gaining this knowledge does not mean we must subscribe to the same ideologies, beliefs, and values handed down for generations. What it means is that this knowledge gives us the footing for who we are and can help us construct our purpose through our identity. As Dr. Martin Luther King, Jr. once stated, we are not the makers of history; we are made by history. Although widely suggested that history is a blueprint for understanding who we are, this book takes the approach that history is the underpinning of who we are that supports our ability to build and grow psychologically, spiritually, physically, and intellectually.

History's Relevance

Throughout history, social circumstances and conditions sparked revolutions and developed revolutionaries. Aristotle described revolutions as cyclical alterations in government practices and policies. From the American and French Revolutions to the Haitian and European Revolutions, the world has seen significant changes by disrupting and defying the established order. Many see revolutions as harmful and destructive forces, particularly in political terms. Yet, for many, revolutions marry righteous anger and cognizant assertiveness that often culminates in drastic, necessary changes. The people who led these movements recognized the importance of self-awareness and self-advocacy.

Revolutionaries advocate radical change in the status quo and are typically people with deep convictions. This trait is an essential indicator of their identity. The actions of early revolutionaries like David Walker, Sojourner Truth, and Frederick Douglass to fight against an inhumane system such as slavery, which confiscated any semblance of individual or group identities for millions of enslaved Africans, suggest their connection to their own identities. As he chronicles his life as a once enslaved man, Douglass (1845) was clear about how important identity was for him in his quest to abolish slavery. He denotes, "I prefer to be true to myself, even at the hazard of incurring the ridicule of others, rather than to be false, and to incur my own abhorrence."[2] This quote is powerful as it applies today, but it is even more compelling considering the conditions under which he lived, even as a free man when Douglass made this statement. These abolitionists lived in a society that did not see or value them. The United States of America deemed African men, women, and children as property, even less appraised than sheep and cattle.

Yet, like many of their ancestors, these early revolutionaries recognized the importance of clinging to their culture, values, and beliefs because if they did not, they would lose the essence of who they were. They understood the detriment that would ensue if they succumbed to the labels placed on them, often equating them to caricatures or sub-humans. Sociologist, historian, and Pan-Africanist civil rights activist W.E.B. Dubois often discussed how Black Americans are born with a veil that shields their identities because the world sees them differently. The veil symbolizes a covering of the inner turmoil experienced with the incessant burden of being Black. Du Bois suggests this "double consciousness"[3] is the two identities most Black people carry living in the United States. The first is a social identity defined by the eyes of the world, often driven by characteristics of "anti" or "other," and the personal identity many early Black folks tried to hold on to and one that Black citizens today try to uncover, discover, and define for themselves.

The obfuscation of Black identity in America began upon their arrival on slave ships in 1619. Africans were savagely removed from their home-lands, stripped of their names, separated from their families, and denied participation in or acknowledgment of any form of cultural rituals. Colo-nizers fed enslaved Africans a religion adapted and modified to maintain white hegemony. The annihilation of Black identity was central to the system of slavery's power and effectiveness. It was vital for America to sustain its white supremacy and inequality practices that enabled them to strengthen its global capital power. Theorist Hortense Spillers explains Black identity in the US as mythical and loaded with prepossessions.[4] These pre-described characterizations of Blackness in America cemented the false idealization of most Black people in America for people world-wide, including Blacks in other regions. So, as early as 1619, as the first Black people arrived in the United States, everything that was done and said was to strip them of any tribal and cultural association attached to their natural identity. Black people have since been fighting against a car-icature identity that does not apply to who they are as a people and cul-ture. The identification of Blackness, defined by more than four hundred years of slavery, is in the foundational structures that form this union. The psychological outcomes of how white folk see and experience Black folk directly result from the practice of slavery. Racism manifests in every aspect of American life, including and significantly in its legislation and laws. In America and many countries worldwide, Blackness is a political construct due to the historical crafting of legislation resulting in outcomes that promote anti-Black, racist laws and policies. These results are directly attributable to how Black people experience life and how others experience them, which for many Black people, influences how they see themselves.

SLAVERY AND AMERICAN IDENTITY

President Lincoln issued the Emancipation Proclamation on January 1, 1863, declaring freedom to all enslaved people living in Confederate states during the Civil War as recourse for those states' rebellion against the Union. This proclamation did not end slavery but helped unite the country in the war. On January 31, 1865, the 13th Amendment, which abolished slavery in the United States, was passed by Congress and ratified by three-fourths of the states on December 6, 1865. In the city of Galveston, in the Confederate state of Texas, Union troops took over and freed all enslaved people on June 19, 1865. This historic day became known as "Juneteenth" and became a US federal holiday on June 15, 2021. The 14th Amendment, which provided citizenship to born and naturalized citizens, including the enslaved, was ratified on July 9, 1868. These legislative actions were crucial in moving America toward its ideal identity that it boasts in its founding documents. National ideals include those in the Declaration of Independence, that "all men are created equal," and all men are endowed to receive "Unalienable Rights" in this country that include "Life, Liberty, and the Pursuit of Happiness."[5] These documents framed the identity of the country's citizens. Citizens (white folk) received their "Unalienable Rights" endowed by their Creator. They were situated at the top of a societal ranking created by the founding principles, values, beliefs, and behaviors of the country's first European settlers. The identity of citizens was associated with their status in society. The system of slavery is the undergirding of the foundational systems established in this country. Therefore, injustice and trauma are the staples in the formation of the culture of America. That foundational hierarchy continues to benefit white people and administer injustice and inequality to non-whites, especially Black citizens. From its founding, the United States has used Blackness as a political construct to hold on to white privilege and a pecking order that manipulates power moves for the country's leaders.

Presumably, President Lincoln was acutely aware of his identity and how his decisions would impact his legacy when he took the position to end slavery. President Lincoln's disdain for slavery is well documented; however, by all accounts, Lincoln's main concern was the "state of the Union." If he could have saved the Union without ending slavery, would he have drafted the Emancipation Proclamation? What do Lincoln's actions or decisions say about who he was or was not? Researchers and scholars make inferences about his intent, but Lincoln's behavior (decisions) provides a framing of his beliefs and values. Many leaders today face similar problems that require them to stand alone, stand firm in their belief and value system, and make decisions that may be detrimental to their power status. Lincoln's identity, framed by the decisions he made, garnered him political power at the same time. Historians and political scientists noted Lincoln's affinity for being self-reflective and contemplative in his decision-making. This inner consciousness undoubtedly guided his decisions. Lincoln's introspection may have given him the confidence to make his aversion to slavery known. During that time, his beliefs could have easily swayed and aligned more with those of the Confederates. But Lincoln examined the system of slavery from a political and financial lens, undoubtedly not escaping the humanistic evaluation. Ultimately, Lincoln's beliefs and actions against the continuation of slavery, that won him the war, cost him his life.

A generation after Lincoln's assassination, almost two million Black Americans left the South to seek opportunities in the North during the Great Migration (1910–1930). This exodus was a turning point for many newly freed enslaved Blacks and their offspring and an opportunity to construct their identities outside the predefined slave narrative. The goal was to elevate their status economically, politically, and socially from enslaved citizens to entrepreneurs, community builders, and revolutionaries. They did this by understanding that they were not what they were called (Nigger). They understood the importance of anchoring their identity in their truth, not the fables, caricatures, and discriminatory descriptors assigned to them to assist in keeping the country's system of chattel slavery and white supremacy in place. Their strength and determination manifested into prosperous enclaves in cities across the country, developing from nothing just one generation after their emancipation from being enslaved. What they accomplished should be celebrated often, especially given where they started. Most history books in US educational systems do not mention the bravery and ingenuity of these revolutionaries who had to imagine and build a life in America beyond the life America had carved for them. Just a generation prior, many of their ancestors were freed from the system of slavery and entered society as freedmen having only the clothes on their backs and a strong belief in self-preservation. Black people had to re-identify who they were, not necessarily for themselves but for people who thought they knew who they were.

The actions of the agitators of chattel slavery are crucial in framing what it was to live under the American system as a Black citizen. Even with barriers before them, many Black people acquired success in America: O.W. Gurley, one of the wealthiest Black men of his time and founder of the Greenwood district in Tulsa, Oklahoma; Rev. William Washington Brown, founder of the mutual aid society, True Reformers, in Richmond, Virginia; John Mitchell, Jr., editor of the Richmond Planet newspaper; and Maggie Lena Walker, the first Black woman bank president (St. Luke Penny Savings Bank) who also ran a newspaper, department store, and life insurance company. These innovators had a framework of who they were and utilized that knowledge to build individual and community wealth. This strong acknowledgment of self and their entrepreneurial prowess signaled a challenge to white supremacists that the pre-defined "societal order" was in jeopardy. During the summer of 1919, historically denoted as "Red Summer," as many as 26 Black enclaves across the country were burned down and bombed, and hundreds of Black citizens were hanged, set on fire, shot, and brutalized.[6] In the name of keeping the identity of America and the structure of its political, economic, and social hierarchy in place, white supremacists destroyed communities and murdered hundreds of Black citizens. When Black people have dared to define themselves for themselves, it has often resulted in death and destruction in this country. These Black pioneers of the past met injustices and racist practices with a determination and brilliance that was, and still is, undeniable and has become a blueprint for today's activists. So, to study history and understand the magnitude of what Black abolitionists, entrepreneurs, and creatives did after the Civil War is imperative for all Americans to know and recognize to understand their individual and collective identities.

RED SUMMER AND THE FRAMING OF BLACK IDENTITY

After the United States Congress passed the 13th Amendment in 1865 to end slavery and involuntary servitude, Blacks were eager to reconstruct their identity beyond the strongholds of the racist stereotypes perpetuated for centuries. In 1914, during the beginning of World War I, Blacks began to migrate from the South into the North to seek labor opportunities as immigration, mainly from Europe, slowed. This departure, known as the Great Migration, allowed Blacks to establish themselves politically, socially, and culturally in many major cities in the North and West. From Oklahoma to Chicago, Blacks built areas where they could live and thrive while fighting for their freedom and democracy.

This period saw a creative explosion in the arts, a sense of self-identity, and awareness that allowed Black people to create socioeconomic havens. Their early efforts resulted in affluent enclaves that would create enormous economic rewards for entire communities. The Greenwood community in Tulsa, Oklahoma, in particular, was deemed one of the wealthiest Black areas in the country. It was referred to as "Black Wall Street" by Booker T. Washington due to its prosperous commerce and numerous successful Black-owned businesses.[7] Greenwood's residents owned over 35 blocks of land, and a growing number of entrepreneurs erected schools, banks, grocery stores, hotels, churches, and dry cleaners for the community to enjoy and to make their neighborhoods self-sustaining. They circulated their dollars at least a hundred times within their neighborhoods, which created a robust system for producing wealth.[8] Black people found a way to coalesce their "double consciousness" into a unified Black identity in these communities.

Unfortunately, the impetus of American racism that escalated into an epidemic of white mob violence marred their progress. "Red Summer" stretched from the late winter through the summer of 1919, when an estimated 26 race riots occurred across the United States, headed by white mobs who targeted Black communities. The violence that took place across several states during Red Summer killed thousands of people. The threat of Black empowerment and advancement and the stereotypes and fears instilled in many white people during this time in history festered this brutality that annihilated Black communities with air attacks, fires, gun raids, and bombings.[9]

Black Wall Street was one of the areas targeted and destroyed. The mere appearance of complicity from local governments in these vile acts intensified the lack of trust Black people had in these agencies. Shortly after that, in 1929, the Great Depression hit the United States, marking the worst economic crisis in its history, further hindering Black people's ability to re-establish themselves financially.[10] This blockage from financial growth opportunities is correlated with how Black people are seen and treated in the US and, undoubtedly, how they see themselves and their communities.

THE HARLEM RENAISSANCE (1918–1929) AND THE AMERICAN DREAM

The 1920s brought about a lot of change in America. Many white Americans were living "high off the hog," as the saying goes, benefitting from the stock market. The Blues influenced Jazz, and women had a sense of sexual freedom. Racism was still prevalent, especially in the South.

Harlem nurtured a sense of pride for African Americans who, for the first time, were living in a community with others who looked like them and shared similar experiences. Many gladly made the pilgrimage from the South, hoping for a better life and job opportunities in the North. The gathering of African Americans in Harlem was a testament to many things. One of the most important was that being a culture was only by name until they dwelled, worked, socialized, and lived amongst themselves. After the Civil War marked the first time Black Americans could merge and strategize about how to become participants and engage in society and build self-sustaining enterprises that would help frame what the Black "American Dream" would look like. During this time, the mass migration of Black Southerners to northern industrial states took place, and Harlem was one of those designated cities. The success of many Black professionals and the formation of the National Association of the Advancement of Colored People (NAACP) drew other Black Americans to New York. Black writers, intellectuals, politicians, musicians, and other artists congregated in Harlem to redefine what it meant and looked like to be Black in America.

Many Black scholars, intellectuals, and creatives recognized the historical destruction of the Black identity, and they wanted to reaffirm, re-establish, and re-construct what it meant to be Black in America outside of the condition of slavery. This reframing happened through the arts. Harlem became where many Black Americans could shed the shackles of the oppressive South, explore who they were, and define their culture for themselves.

But the Harlem Renaissance did not stop the societal stereotypes that situated Black people as buffoons and unintelligent, specifically in the media with roles such as "Jim Crow," "Zip Coon," and others. Society projected theatrical and film depictions onto all Black people in America. Once again, Black citizens had to work against these ideologies while simultaneously trying to understand and define who they were for themselves. Only within the last few decades have these images been countered with positive images that have begun to pierce stereotypical characteristics and ideas of Black Americans.

Many Black leaders during the Harlem Renaissance were re-establishing what it meant to be Black in America. Through art, poetry, music, theatre, movies, and politics, Black people had pathways to the "Black American Dream" and unraveling the chains of enslavement from their identity for themselves and non-Black Americans. The "Black American Dream" is a derivative of "The American Dream" because Black people still do not have as full access to resources and opportunities as white Americans, even when they work harder and are more credentialed.

Blackness, used as a political construct, anchored the historical trauma for Black people perpetrated through American systems. The dichotomy of being Black and American has created a burden for many Black people who constantly fight against the stereotypical narratives while developing and framing their own identity outside of what American systems have deemed them to be. The American melting pot is a metaphor and something to strive for, but the country is far from embodying this premise. Cultural, ethnic, and racial differences have proven to be the impetus for many of America's problems.

For Black Americans, knowing American history is detrimental to navigating and living in this country and establishing identities conducive to their values, beliefs, and generational traditions that form who they are and desire to be.

Historical Social Constructs and their Impact on Identity

The socio-historical implications of one's identity are essential to the structure of one's identity. The social bases of identity intersect with race, gender, ethnicity, class, and age. Research continues to suggest that actions and behaviors frame the constitution of identity. Sociologists and social psychologists view identity as an intersection between personal and social experiences and behaviors. Adapting to social environments influences individual choices and can change or alter self-awareness. Historically, societal norms and structures changed how people saw themselves. For instance, when the system of slavery began, African traditions, which are customs, behavioral practices, and actions passed down through generations, were stripped from them. They had to mask their beliefs and values to survive. Thus, they altered who they were, and this shift became permanent for many. Identity is not static; it is fluid. The foundation weakening of identity can be swift or happen over time until there is no recollection of or resemblance to who you once were.

Society, for some, has a significant impact on identity. Our social groups and memberships can influence values, behaviors, and attitudes away from innate beliefs. Historical influences can also alter culturally based identities. Societal identity aligns with how you are seen and treated; there may be a natural inclination to adjust and restructure your identity to make it more conducive to the groups and communities that are valued more. This shift is undoubtedly true for marginalized people based on society's hierarchy constructs. The struggle against social inequalities, which for far too many is a daily fight, can invade the psyche of those constantly fighting for justice. This identity alteration is also valid for those in privileged positions who may see themselves as the keeper of a societal order from which they benefit. Psychological research suggests that identity reflects what has happened and is currently happening in society.

Capitalism and Identity

Many historians argue that the idea of identity in earlier times was more of an assignment than a unique formation. Family heritage and ethnic and racial traditions significantly influence a person's standing in society and how one sees oneself. An individual's standing in society was an indicator of their socioeconomic group, and membership in a social group indicated how people saw themselves and how society saw and treated them.[11] Money and wealth have always been specific measures of success, a determination of human value, which are significant characteristics of American identity and idealism. Those who have wealth can obtain all that America has to offer. Those who do not, specifically those in marginalized communities, lack the access and resources necessary to fully embrace America's notion of independence and equality for every citizen, defined by life, liberty, and the pursuit of happiness.

Indeed, this ideal is only attainable were capitalism to work for everyone equally, which it does not. History shows that capitalism cannot work without poverty and oppression. The necessity for social classes is indicated by and cemented in our laws and policies that perpetuate this imbalance.

The US economy experienced phenomenal growth after World War II; labor workers moved from housing tenements into single-family housing. Although many Black families had to move into these housing projects, there were still thriving Black communities around the country, such as

Seneca Village in New York City, now the home of Central Park. It did not take long before the abuse of Black people started again, this time by federal policies. The federal government aggressively utilized its eminent domain power to acquire and redistribute land supporting New Deal policies. The Assistant Attorney General at the time called the Lands Division of the government "the biggest real estate office of any time or place."[12] These events and public policy laws, such as Jim Crow, resulted in the devastating housing crisis that would have lasting economic, social, and political effects on Black communities.[13] Public policies can hinder or improve citizens' lives, and how people live tremendously impacts their identity. Historically, policies have not had a positive outcome in the US for Black citizens and other marginalized groups, and this has lasting effects.

The historical implication of policy sets an important precedent that is still prevalent in many communities today, and that is the lack of trust. A steep precipice has formed between many marginalized Black communities and the government due to the apparent systematic inequality of housing laws that have historically impeded their progress.[14] The literature on African Americans' political trust has chiefly addressed the roles that descriptive (based on similar social characteristics) and substantive (based on similar policy interests) representation play in enhancing African Americans' political trust.[15] Distrust in any realm can inhibit the functioning of most elements of society and disrupt measures that could produce effective community engagement. Beyond the political constructs, some research studies have treated "trust,"' in general within Black communities, as a culturally determined primitive. Understanding the determinants of trust within marginalized Black areas could be prudent in assessing how these communities respond to policies that improve their individual and collective lives. Limited research has been conducted on trust and how Black citizens see their value in society as translating into how they see and value themselves.

Race, racism, and discrimination are constructs that every President of the United States has had to confront due to their impact on the country's economy. Since Lincoln's Emancipation Proclamation, legislators and community activists have fought to align the country's racial dynamics toward a more equitable and just society. However, the pull of normalcy toward the foundational identity of the government continues to hinder progress. White citizens' freedom to live in this society and access all its resources and opportunities is enormous compared to the freedom and access of Blacks and other marginalized citizens. Although there is a tremendous weight put on economic status in this country, poor non-Blacks statistically have always been in a better position in society overall than poor Blacks, who may be better off financially. Poor non-Blacks have better access to resources and, unlike non-white citizens, are not constrained by some of the social injustices that derail or block the potential for Blacks to elevate themselves out of their current economic standing and positions.

This economic tug-of-war dates back to slavery. Early in the establishment of American society, it was prudent not to be on the bottom of the economic totem pole. The proponents of slavery justified its position as a social system that would always have Black, enslaved laborers in the last place in the country's social hierarchy. The outcome of this system created an intense racial and class division that persists today across race, gender, and political ideologies and cultures. Some poor whites, enticed by privilege under white supremacy, even found a way to enslave people to their financial detriment. Poor whites' identity was tied to elite whites through their shared cultural and religious heritage. This connection made it easier for poor whites to live in and navigate the American system and allowed them opportunities to help them elevate their way to a higher social class. Their identity was not solely defined by and restricted to their socio-economic position. In contrast, Black people's identity, seen by non-Black citizens, was explicitly tied to the racist and discriminatory depictions that fueled the system of slavery and the falsehood of white supremacy. This characterization has been normalized and passed down for centuries.

History and the Current Debate

In his speech at the National Press Club in 1986, James Baldwin expressed the influence of history on how we live our lives today.

> One of the things that has always afflicted the American reality and the American vision is the aversion to history. History is not something you read about in a book: history is not even the past, it's the present, because everybody operates, whether or not we know it, out of assumptions that are produced only, and only by, our history.[16]

In addition to their economic and political constraints, Black people had to be mindful of their physical and emotional well-being of "living while Black" in this country. Black Americans must question whether their hair is offensive to white people in the workplace and social settings. They must discern if their clothes are too ethnic, if they have too much bounce in their walk, or if they use the correct language and have the right tone so no one is offended or made to feel uncomfortable. To not have to question these things is indeed a privilege. Black and brown people are in jeopardy of losing their livelihood, freedom, or even their life if they make certain white folk uncomfortable. Often, Black Americans must decide whether they will "play the game." This participation means shelving much of their "Blackness" to assimilate into the dominant culture so that they have a greater chance at "success" within systems designed to disjoin them from the rest of society and certainly seclude them from opportunities for advancement. This burden of being non-white in the US has traversed generations and significantly impacted Black identity.

Black citizens are not the only ones impacted by these racist systemic attitudes and practices. All of society suffers from denying equal opportunity to freedom for any citizen or cultural group and preventing them from their pursuit of happiness. The system of slavery created a distinct identity for America that still informs its citizens and people worldwide. Many Americans would like to erase America's founding principles of chattel slavery. Still, the residue of its existence is steeped in the country's current laws and inherent in its citizens' generational values and behaviors toward Black people.

Some top political leaders have tried to legislate away the brutal lynching, violence, and injustices that happened to over 300 million Africans for over 400 years by politicizing and policing what children should learn in school. This practice was evident in the recent backlash against The 1619 Project, an ongoing initiative from *The New York Times Magazine*, and the banishing of critical race theory (CRT), an academic and legal framework mainly taught in law schools and graduate research-based programs. Conservative politicians have utilized "wokeness," being aware of social injustice and discriminatory practices, and CRT as tools to push their agendas. Florida's governor Ron DeSantis' incessant policy attacks on Black Floridians continue with his efforts to white-wash American history by banning African American studies modules from the State's high school Advanced Placement program. He is also pushing the narrative that Black enslaved people benefited from slavery due to the skills they acquired during the 400+ years of enslavement and inhumane treatment. DeSantis' narrative ignores the fact that enslaved Africans stolen from their land were skilled farmers and craftsmen. Unfortunately, DeSantis is not alone. The governors of Arkansas and Georgia have limited history classes and lessons about slavery because it makes white students feel guilty. This further alienates Black citizens and sends a message that they, and the hundreds of years of torture and trauma their ancestors endured, do not matter. DeSantis' concern that white children will feel guilty ignores and disregards the feelings of Black children who often suffer in silence, carrying the trauma of their ancestors and living under the country's history of racism.

Interestingly, even though CRT is non-existent in K-12 education, politicians have re-defined this theory to push forward a far-right political agenda to white-wash American history by eliminating any remnants of the evil and inhumane practices of slavery. CRT has become a catcall for everything the far right dictates as anti-American, divisive, or racially charged. Mandating and legislating a rule to ignore factual historical events and conventions in American history will continue to be detrimental to the construction of white identity in the United States. White supremacy is rooted in the diluting and entire erasure of Black contributions and Black excellence. America's systems of government, plagued by its anchoring of racism, continue to affect Black and brown citizens in their everyday lives. Ignoring the history of the United States will never erase slavery, the Black Codes, Jim Crow laws, and the criminalization of Blackness because these foundational beliefs, legislative practices, and regulations are inherent in the country's fabric.

The US can still construct an identity that acknowledges its bloody history. To reconcile the past and live up to its promises in its founding documents for all its citizens, America's recognition of the system of slavery and the terror it inflicted for over 400 years on millions of Africans would be a great starting place. The acknowledgment of this period's political, economic, educational, and social gains delivered to white people, and the continuous privilege bestowed on them and their generations, would also situate the country's standing with its Black citizens. At the very minimum, the government must give retribution to its Black citizens through a full confession of the wrongs it has inflicted on our ancestors and how these continue to plague our community generations later. After the campaigns against critical race theory and Black Lives Matter, some American leaders have historically recognized the seismic shift the truth can have on the normalized, foundational order of power in this country.

The strength and innovativeness of the Native Americans and the first Africans to arrive on US soil must have played a vital part in those first Europeans arriving here to establish a pecking order and legislate the continuum of a white supremacy societal hierarchy. These early congressmen made it illegal for Black people, Africans, to keep their names and families, read and learn, or gather as a group. Why? Why was it vital for them to keep the Black identity as an inhuman caricature? The settlers knew even back then that once a person is clear and aware of who they are, it is nearly impossible to manipulate them and alter their values, beliefs, attitudes, and behaviors. Many of the revolts that happened during enslavement were the result of Black people holding onto their identities and understanding who they were and from whence they came. Arguably, when leaders seek an understanding of their history – personal, social, state, and the world, research suggests that it strengthens their situational awareness and provides valuable insight into the ramifications of their decisions, and how crises may ignite.

Significant empirical data supports the importance of history's long-term effects on economic, political, social, and environmental development. History empowers those who want to engage to be better informed to understand the ever-changing world that ultimately informs who we are. History is generally taught in one dimension, with memorization as the essential skill set to progress successfully. However, history should not be about memorization. Contextual analysis of the past is necessary to explore and plan. In this climate of immediacy and the Internet, information is often challenged and manipulated to fit an ideological and political position.

Leaders who examine previous crises and the outcomes from past decisions position themselves to handle current problems and situations effectively because of the information retrieved. History can provide essential tools such as crisis management, conflict resolution, and relationship building, which strengthen one's resilience and confidence professionally and personally. Conflicts today, when dissected, have deep historical roots that can provide the key to solutions. This benefit is true in every role a leader may hold. Citizens of every walk of life should take the time to understand their histories at every level. When we begin to unravel those generational triggers and ideologies that are beholden to the past and those unconscious beliefs and values that do not align with equity and justice for everyone, then as a nation and as a world, we can begin to mend those deep sores that the events of history have inflicted. These wounds could be the guilt that Governor DeSantis seeks to hide from white children in his state due to the colonizing history of their forefathers, or these inflictions could be the trauma and residual systemic practices that Black people in America must contend with in everyday life. For healing to be possible, complete and truthful accounts of history must be told and acknowledged. Instead of moving in the direction of historical paralysis, history can be a valuable source for forward movement in race relations, economic equity, and equal access to education and employment.

Summary

History plays a significant role in this leadership framework in helping leaders assess who they are and aspire to be. History is the foundation of identity and is crucial in current behaviors, attitudes, and values. History is something to remember. In the bible, Ecclesiastes 1 verse 9 states, "What has been will be again, what has been done will be done again; there is nothing new under the sun." This verse sums up the importance of knowing history. The information in this chapter may not be historical events pertinent to every leader's identity revolutionary journey. Each leader should reflect and discern which historical incidents have impacted their identity and whether any changes or modifications in behaviors, attitudes, values, or ideologies need to happen to reach their aspirational selves.

Notes

1 Eddyhrbs. (2012). Builder's engineer info. Retrieved January 12, 2023, from http://www.buildersengineer.info/
2 Douglass, F., Andrews, W. L., & McFeely, W. S. (1997). *Narrative of the Life of Frederick Douglass: Authoritative Text, Contexts, Criticism*. W.W. Norton & Co.

3 Du Bois, W. E. B. (2022). *The Souls of Black Folk*. Berkshire Publishing Group
4 Spillers, H. J. (1987). Mama's Baby, Papa's Maybe: An American Grammar Book. *JSTOR, 17*(2), 64–81.
5 National Archives and Records Administration. (n.d.). *Declaration of Independence: A Transcription*. Retrieved November 27, 2022, from https://www.archives.gov/founding-docs/declaration-transcript
6 National Archives and Records Administration. (n.d.). *Racial Violence and the Red Summer*. Retrieved November 27, 2022, from https://www.archives.gov/research/african-americans/wwi/red-summer
7 Wilson, J. J. (1999). *The Black Wallstreet: Historical Files Study Guide: "The Bombing of America's Most Affluent Black Community."* Black Wallstreet Publ. Group.
8 Messer, C. M. (2021). Greenwood: The Rise and Devastation of "Black Wall Street." *The 1921 Tulsa Race Massacre*, 21–32. https://doi.org/10.1007/978-3-030-74679-7_2
9 Hodges, A. J. (2013). The Red Summer of 1919: Toward a Synthesis – Cameron McWhirter. Red Summer: The Summer of 1919 and the Awakening of Black America. New York: Henry Holt, 2011. 368 pp. $32.50 (cloth), ISBN 978-0-8050-8906-6; $16.99 (paper), ISBN 978-1-4299-7293-2. *The Journal of the Gilded Age and Progressive Era, 12*(1), 141–144. https://doi.org/10.1017/s1537781412000576
10 Messer, C. M., Shriver, T. E., & Adams, A. E. (1970, January 1). The Destruction of Black Wall Street: Tulsa's 1921 Riot and the Eradication of Accumulated Wealth. *American Journal of Economics and Sociology*. Retrieved April 25, 2023, from https://econpapers.repec.org/RePEc:bla:ajecsc:v:77:y:2018:i:3-4:p:789-819
11 Bloxham, D. (2020). History, Identity, and the Present. *History and Morality*, 251–290. https://doi.org/10.1093/oso/9780198858713.003.0005
12 Justice.gov. (2022, January 24). *History of the Federal Use of Eminent Domain*. The United States Department of Justice. Retrieved April 29, 2023, from https://www.justice.gov/enrd/history-federal-use-eminent-domain#:~:text=During%20World%20War%20II%2C%20the,United%20States%20145%20F.
13 Kravetz, N. (2018). United States Educational Policies and Black Cultural Identity. *Cultural Identity and Educational Policy*, 286–303. https://doi.org/10.4324/9780429503771-13
14 Herring, C., & Henderson, L. (2016). Wealth Inequality in Black and White: Cultural and Structural Sources of the Racial Wealth Gap. *Race and Social Problems, 8*(1), 4–17. https://doi.org/10.1007/s12552-016-9159-8
15 Mangum, M. (2011). Explaining Political Trust Among African Americans: Examining Demographic, Media, Social Capital and Social Networks Effects. *The Social Science Journal, 48*(4), 589–596. https://doi.org/10.1016/j.soscij.2011.03.002
16 Vogel, J. (2018). *James Baldwin and the 1980s: Witnessing the Reagan Era*. University of Illinois Press. https://doi.org/10.5406/j.ctv6p4dx

Chapter 4

Phase II

The Framing – Theoretical Framework

Epigenetics and Psychology

For decades, epigenetic research has provided important information toward advancing agriculture, medicine, species conservation, heredity, and evolution. Scientists have found that epigenetic inheritance systems use non-DNA variations to transmit cell and organism lineages that alter genetic behavior without changing DNA. Epigenetics studies have indicated how the environment and behaviors can change the natural genetic functionality within one's DNA. Trauma has been linked explicitly to this genetic transference due to a chemical alteration of a person's genes. Genetic characteristics are expressed, active, suppressed, or unexpressed, based on environmental factors such as stress and trauma. As humans, our DNA – genome – is 99% the same.[1] The minimal differences in our DNA and our unique environmental experiences make us unique. Everything that we do can essentially trigger epigenetic molecules to attach to a DNA cell and instruct that segment to bypass or ignore the gene that may be present in that DNA. Drug use, stress, nutrition, neglect, social contact, environmental complexities, exercise, and trauma can alter genetic makeup, shifting behavior, attitudes, values, or beliefs. One's environment and heredity are connected and constantly interact. Epigenetics and DNA are central to why SLIM's framework anchors the re-identity process by connecting with and understanding how history and memory help to frame leadership identity. Understanding behaviors, emotions, and habits, possibly genetically transferred, that appear based on potentially genetically transmitted triggers are helpful indicators of one's schematic leadership framework.

Transgenerational behaviors and ideologies have rich research supporting them via epigenetics and DNA transference. Sigmund Freud's theory of psychoanalysis uncovers resiliency and grievance from the familial unconscious passed down through generations.[2] It cannot be overstated that identifying and reclaiming one's history and memories is essential to frame an identity. Parsing generational trauma and addressing social and

DOI: 10.4324/9781003394051-4

racial attitudes that many attribute to deeply uncovered feelings and ideologies are vital to changing unflattering behavior that does not align with one's desired self. The study of the psyche often considers a generational analysis of traits and behaviors. Interestingly, examinations of historical atrocities – American chattel slavery, the psychological outcomes of war, the Holocaust, ethnic genocides, the Chinese cultural revolution, the Armenian massacre, and the displacements of Koreans – have significant research in this regard. Psychologists and health care providers posit that Post Traumatic Stress Disorder (PTSD) has heritability qualities passed down through generations, much like other psychiatric and mental disorders and illnesses.[3] This research only strengthens the idea that generations of descendants of enslaved Africans can have transgenerational trauma due to chattel slavery and the ongoing injustices and discrimination that continue to occur due to racism. Generations after these horrifying incidents, people in these cultural, ethnic, racial, and gender target groups have visceral reactions and feelings when hearing and speaking about these events because, as studies suggest, terror, horror, fear, and trauma live within their DNA.

Research has found that those social dynamics and experiences that are difficult to emote and effectively unbearable to process are in the unconscious psyche of the next generations. The outcome of this transference is typically a sensitivity to that event or experience. As mentioned, this is like the traits and reactions of veterans with PTSD. For many Black communities and Black families, inter- and transgenerational trauma passed down, like other cultures pass down real estate and financial inheritances. Enduring traumas make healing difficult. Studies in behavioral transference identify a process of the heritage associated with biology. Unconscious conflicts and attitudes might be primed genetically and coerced into manifestation when faced with psychological challenges that tap into unconscious knowledge.[4] Scientific advancements continue in DNA transference of traumatic memories through multiple generations, specifically on the maternal gene line. Studies explore the early environmental exposures of the offspring in the womb and during postnatal care. Due to the complexity of human studies and the methodological challenges of conducting research in this area, researchers have not confirmed intergenerational effects of trauma attributed to a single set of biological genes. Yet, intergenerational effects shown via generational studies provide information regarding the impact cogent knowledge of cultural, societal, and individual experiences have on intergenerational transmission.[5] Much research has been conducted on this phenomenon regarding the trauma passed down from the Holocaust. However, minimal research has been conducted on the transgenerational transference of trauma passed down from centuries of horrific experiences from chattel slavery.

Post Traumatic Slave Syndrome (PTSS), a term coined by Dr. Joy DeGruy, and according to her website (joydegruy.com), describes the condition as a theory that explains the causes of several adaptive survival behaviors in Black American communities throughout the United States and the Diaspora. Dr. DeGruy suggests that this condition is a consequence of the centuries of chattel slavery and its oppressive outcomes on the inter- and transgenerational Africans and their descendants. Chattel slavery differed from indentured servitude and earlier forms of slavery, a form of debt bondage. Chattel slavery considered enslaved Africans property, not valued human beings. The premise of this system of slavery was that Black people were genetically and inherently inferior to whites. This ideology was the impetus for the hatred and brutal treatment of millions of Africans over centuries and is the framing of the systems that Black Americans still live under today in the United States. Dr. DeGruy's research of PTSS suggests the infliction of institutionalized racism that perpetuates ongoing injury to Black lives results in a construct she denotes as MAP:

M – Multigenerational trauma, together with continued oppression
A – Absence of opportunity to heal or access the benefits available in society that leads to
P – Post Traumatic Slave Syndrome

According to Dr. DeGruy, PTSS, and PTSD diagnoses can align in the following ways:

- Certain places, people, events, or activities can trigger traumatic experiences in individuals.
- Depression, feeling emotionally numb or vacant, and a general self-destructive and hopeless outlook on life.

Although these triggers indicate PTSS, some trauma may reveal itself more subtly, sometimes unrecognizable as trauma.[6] Terrie Williams, the author of *Black Pain: It Just Looks Like We're Not Hurting*, offers a first-hand account of what deep depression can look like due to the Black experience in America. The normalcy of Black pain expressed in this book is not prescriptive as she urges her readers to examine and acknowledge the source of our pain so that a solution can be remedied. The consequences of unchecked trauma cannot be understated. People who may seem to handle emotional and psychological wounds and injury well are often suffering in silence and susceptible to deep depression, according to Williams and other psychologists.[7]

People in the African diaspora can innately sense the system of violence that led to the traumatizing conditions perpetrated against Black people during the transatlantic slave trade and the inheritance of trauma from 400 years of enslavement that has led to the current systemic traumatization and physical brutality of Black bodies. The distrust and the impact of trauma, generation to generation, according to epigenetic researchers, can be inherent in the gene pools of Black people.[8]

Personal Revolutions

Cultural and social relationships and affiliations play an essential role in constructing identity. Although many people want to believe they are immune to societal norms and what others may say or think of them, these associations matter. The stories we tell about this country are crucial because they impact the stories we tell about ourselves. The historical events discussed in this chapter may seem unrelated to the identity discussion for this book, however, to the contrary; this history has significance not only to Black identity but to American identity, which influences individual leadership identity. National and cultural identities are significant for leaders in regions throughout the world. How leaders identify themselves – within social groups, in generational ideologies, habits, and behaviors, and who they aspire to be– is instrumental in making decisions.

America is not alone in its dangerous and violent history that birthed revolutionaries. Toussaint L'Ouverture was a fierce leader who led what many historians have called the "greatest revolt against slavery"[9] in the Haitian Revolution of 1791. L'Ouverture's strong self-determination moved him from slave herdsman to French general and then governor of Saint-Domingue, Haiti. Mahatma Gandhi led India's independence from imperial Britain with his nonviolent resistance movement. His extreme self-actualization of personal peace manifested the political ideology of Gandhi. Ernesto "Che" Guevara was a compassionate, fierce liberation fighter with a heart for Cuba's people. He became a symbol of democratic expression and a visionary of radical dissent.

These notables arrived at their revolutionary humanism at different points in their lives for various reasons. But historians disagree about whether they all arrived at a point of understanding something about themselves. They chose to do what they did because of an urging, a skill, a gift, or a fierce determination that could aid their movements. There was something in them that gave them the drive to fight, change the trajectory of injustice, and suffer for themselves and their fellow compatriots. There must have been a self-discovery, an awakening, a transformation that gave them the fortitude to push through. The common thread with these revolutionaries and many others is that they had an awakening period. This arousal is the process of beginning a personal revolution.

Historians and scholars attest that social, economic, political, technological, and personal revolutions can create profound and sometimes radical transformations that alter the status quo. Personal revolutions invoke a shift in one's mindset. Unlike social and political revolutions, personal revolutions are not bombastic and public. These changes are often gradual and noticeable over time. The power of any process that changes norms is its ability to constitute a sustainable change of behavior that results in "better" outcomes. A deep and honest reflection of self identifies ideal results that align with our aspirational core selves. But what is the meaning of the core self? How can someone tap into it? When will they know that they have? The core self is an overall view of who we say we are. Our beliefs, values, and attitudes are born in the core self. Much of who we are is indicative of our generational heredity and the stories told to us. Our histories and memories are important markers and indicators of how to adjust and move in the future. For some, looking back is painful and meaningless. But history often holds clues to the answers that will help heal and provide knowledge that clarifies things.

Identity is a multi-layered dynamic construct framed by social and cultural influences and genetic characteristics. Inter- and transgenerational traits, attitudes, and behaviors passed down could be significant indicators of one's identity. History has become a political weapon politicians use to push personal agendas to hide the truth to align with historical racist and discriminatory practices. Legislation recently passed to remove certain historical events from school systems suggests that offering America's complete and accurate history would harm white children because the truth would make them feel guilty. These politicians believe teaching students about African enslaved people is not problematic, but instructing these students about the people who created this evil, inhumane, and brutal system is where they draw the line. Some public servants continue to ignore the ongoing trauma inflicted on Black children who see the horrendous images of their ancestors who were treated worse than cattle.

For white Americans, research suggests, this country's legacy of white supremacy and racist ideology has the potential to transmit in their DNA from their ancestors as well. The incomprehensible treatment of enslaved Africans will forever be a part of many Black Americans' genetic makeup. Indeed, not everyone believes that we carry psychological and experiential factors from our bloodline, but significant research suggests it is plausible and probable. Some scholars of Epigenetics, social scientists, and historians believe this trauma transfers through many generations.[10] The historical culture of America embedded in policies, laws, and ideologies adds another layer of transference that makes it difficult to penetrate and escape historical tropes that influence behavior and attitudes.

Uncovering the source of unwanted behaviors requires deep reflection, which is a laborious exercise. This discovery requires a willingness and commitment to honesty. The roots of implicit and unconscious bias are rooted in generational traditions passed down and experiences tucked away in parts of our consciousness that are not easily retrievable (unconscious). The more time invested in looking at ourselves and reflecting on memories connected to certain behaviors, values, and beliefs, the more succinct our identity becomes.

Unconscious and Implicit Bias

Some people may believe that their "unconscious bias" is not a part of their identity schema, when in fact, it is the anchoring of identity. Some cognitive and perceptual psychologists believe the unconscious mind is where processes exist that automatically influence conscious thought and behavior. The unconscious is the layer of the mind that is not easily accessible for introspection, and so is at the core of the natural self. Historically, social scientists have defined the unconscious as unintentional, subliminal, and restrictive, but with new research, many are moving away from this narrative. In the past few decades, some social psychologists' views on the unconscious mind have differed from traditional cognitive psychologists' perspectives. Research now informs that the unconscious mind is a pervasive and powerful influence over other mental processes.[11] Current studies conclude that the unconscious mind precedes the conscious mind. The emphasis shifts from unconscious cognitive processes to unconscious stimuli.[12]

Unconscious and implicit bias can stem from classical conditioning, where something (stimulus) invokes an unwanted response (behavior). Conditioning could arise from inter or transgenerational ideologies, values, or beliefs passed down that are not at the surface of one's consciousness or triggered by a specific experience or memory embedded in the preconscious or unconscious. These biases can also have direct societal implications. Policies and legislation that assert characteristics of certain groups have lasting effects on how society treats those groups. Segregation, redlining, other housing and banking policies, mass incarceration, and the consistent lack of accountability for police killing unarmed Black people play an essential part in society's treatment and perceptions of Black people. In her many years of research, Dr. Jennifer Eberhardt has examined the root causes of unconscious bias and its effects on society. Much of her research has uncovered how the brain is inclined to categorize things based on stimuli, which can lead to baseless assumptions and discrimination due to anxiety, stress, and worry.[13]

Researchers have long suggested the power of the unconscious to influence behavior. Hidden memories, habits, repressed thoughts, desires, and repressed feelings motivate our actions. Every interaction and daily experience comes with expectations that tap into the mind's unconscious. Social scientists now attribute reflexive reactions to how we unconsciously perceive and react to people. Understanding the unconscious mind requires acknowledging and identifying impulses in our behaviors and emotions that are difficult to control. Many people want to disassociate themselves from their unconscious mind and behaviors, but as research suggests, the unconscious significantly influences our decisions and attitudes.

We must understand how the unconscious can exert itself on our behavior and the difficulty in acknowledging and controlling certain impulses. Being able to regulate our behavior—whether making friends, getting up to speed at a new job, or overcoming a drinking problem—depends on more than genes, temperament, and social support networks. It also hinges, in no small measure, on our capacity to identify and try to overcome the automatic impulses and emotions that influence every aspect of our waking life. These emotions run deep and as some research offers, result from our inter- and transgenerational histories and experiences of our ancestors. To make our way in the world, we must understand, acknowledge, and change the outcomes of our unconscious selves in some circumstances.

SLIM's research suggests that the conscious levels of memory are a psychological phenomenon, not a neuroanatomical structure. Therefore, the framing of consciousness for these exercises is a mental structuring that deals with our levels of awareness and how they dictate self-control and, ultimately, our actions. Unconscious and implicit biases are a part of your schematic identity. Like other behaviors and habits, they should not be excused and dismissed if they do not align with your "being." You are ultimately accountable for your actions and are responsible for eliminating them from your identity model. Uncovering and exposing deeply rooted memories can be emotional and troubling and sometimes requires the support of professional therapy or counseling. This workbook does not lend itself to replacing this type of professional assistance. Still, it provides an additional tool to learn how your history and memory affect who you are and want to be.

Your conscious and preconscious memories, thoughts, values, and ideologies that undergird your habits and behaviors are more "black and white" regarding their roots than those in your unconsciousness. However, just because the unconscious may be more difficult and time-consuming to identify does not mean it is not a central part of your identity. The best practice for this workbook is to revisit the journal entries and exercises over time. This repetition allows you to uncover those unwanted values and beliefs that derive from unconscious and implicit biases. Each application provides an opportunity to go deeper into your experiences and memories. Give yourself grace and understand that everyone has things to work on and work through for their identity journey. The SLIM process is personal and something that only you can do. You must define yourself for yourself, and this journal provides the tools to do just that!

Implicit and unconscious bias can also develop from social and political constructs often inherent in communities and cultures and manifest through systems and laws that people with these biases govern. Hence, since the beginning, America's "melting pot" was derived from a forcible engagement of the settler's defined ideology.

SLIM is a framework developed to assist leaders in understanding who they are and why they think, act, and behave the way they do. This evolutionary process can effectively change your attitudes and behaviors because it comes from within and represents changes you deem necessary. Unconscious bias is the manifestation of something already in you that comes through to your conscious self. SLIM offers strategies to understand how generational beliefs, behaviors, patterns, thoughts, and actions show up in what you do and how you see the world. This model helps guide you on your journey of self-discovery to re-evaluate, redefine, and reposition your leadership identity.

As most of us work tirelessly to meet the goals and objectives of our company's mission and vision, this journal helps to support leaders on their quest to fulfill their mission and vision for their leadership identity, which is the most potent force of a human being. To know and understand our history is not to mimic it but to use it as a foundation to re-evaluate, redefine, and reposition your identity.

Assimilation vs. Acculturation

Identity's connection to one's potential for success too often depends on how well someone can navigate spaces. This relationship drives many to conform by any means necessary to society's acceptable labeling of who they are and can be. Africans were brutalized and tortured into living within the defined social environment established by enslavers. Africans were not the first group that the American settlers tried to indoctrinate with their beliefs and practices, ultimately brutalizing them physically and destroying communities and their way of living. President Andrew Jackson, the seventh President of the United States, signed the Indian Removal Act on May 28, 1830. This legislation enabled him to forcibly remove Native Americans from lands within the state borders of Georgia, Alabama, North Carolina, Florida, and Tennessee and give Native Americans land west of the Mississippi, land now designated as Oklahoma.[14] After unsuccessfully trying to transform tribes into identifying solely with the European way of life, the US government created conflict with Native Americans resulting in the loss of lives and the confiscation of land. Many Native Americans were clear as to who they were and would not acquiesce to the will of the European settlers via their "cultural" perspectives, values, and beliefs.

The pull to assimilate is strong in the US and many countries around the world, but this can result in losing the customs, traditions, and values of one's culture. The dissipation of part of one's identity should not be required to live and thrive in a free society. But it is, and thus, the impetus for some Black people, and people from other cultures and ethnicities to code-switch. Code-switching changes behavior, speech, appearance, and style to appease others and receive opportunities and fair treatment. America presents a unique problem for cultures and ethnicities that wish to maintain their unique identities, which ultimately delivers a challenge for individuals that belong to those groups. And specifically for Black Americans, the dichotomy of being Black and American and the framing of Blackness historically represents the invisibility of individualism denoting a monolithic culture, which is far from the truth.

Nevertheless, this ideology is prevalent worldwide, for Black people and cultures and other cultures and ethnicities who must assimilate into their mainstream societies. History, again, gives insight into the outcomes of behaviors, attitudes, ideologies, and values. Black people may have thought assimilation would appease the contempt of white folk who despised their existence. Ultimately the infiltration of racism in policies and practices outweighed any willingness to make others comfortable. Author, activist, and playwright, Lorraine Hansberry, wrote about the struggles of assimilation:

> As a child of the Black élite, she wrote, she had been taught how to dress and act for the "dominant social group." It had not changed which hotels would deny her entrance or stopped the cops from sneering at her mother when a brick shattered her window. Appeasement, Hansberry believed, wouldn't get you very far. Her demand was freedom, nothing less.[15]

Hansberry was not alone in her reflective analysis. Many Black people throughout history recognized that racism did not adhere to the rules of assimilation, which is a dual process of change.

On the other hand, acculturation was seemingly more of the goal of American settlers for every ethnic group except Africans. Acculturation happens when the minority culture changes to assimilate into the majority culture but retains some semblance of its cultural heritage. Italian Americans, Jewish Americans, Asian Americans, and Latin/Hispanic Americans have all held on to their native language, cultural markers, food, and customs. Much of the Native Americans' tribal land was stolen; some tribes lost their cultural traditions, and some retained their culture and traditions. For Africans who were stolen from their lands and brought to America, colonizers immediately stripped them of their language, customs, and cultural practices with no chance of preservation.

Social Cognitive Theory

As resilient and steadfast as many enslaved Africans were to keep their tribal traditions and cultural heritage, the centuries-long depictions of who they are have inevitably penetrated some part of their psyche. The treatment of the poor and marginalized worldwide often impacts their idea of self. Social cognitive theory is the influence of individual experiences, environmental factors, and the actions of others on one's ideation of self and others.[16] This theory underpins the formation of personalities and the significance of social observation. Social positions and classifications have immediate consequences on how we see ourselves. Our social categorization systems play an impactful role in the perception and justification of social relationships, which indicates how our social identities embed sociopolitical and sociohistorical contexts.[17]

Social cognition includes the development of schemas or organized knowledge about oneself. These schemas are cognitive versions of our characteristics, behaviors, and attitudes that make up our identity, which is an anchoring feature for SLIM. Social identity theory's social and personal dimensions interplay in developing our identity. Social psychologists argue that self-esteem is enhanced by social status because people often evaluate themselves and those around them positively while assessing those in the out-group negatively.

Social Identity Theory

Henri Tajfel's (1970) social identity theory (SIT) helps explain individual behaviors based on their associations with the groups they belong to.[18] These relationships constitute behaviors based on differences within groups and outside the group. SIT has been used extensively in research studies to identify the relevance of membership to behavior, even among cultural and ethnic groups.

Diversity, equity, and inclusion (DEI) is a hot issue currently in businesses across all sectors. More and more leaders are recognizing that, with access to more information, the world's boundaries are shrinking, and people see each other differently. Typically, SIT is leveraged to understand and acknowledge group dynamics for those in the out-groups and give members in the in-group a sense of comfort and belonging. Again, not all groups benefit from this prescription.

As mentioned earlier, this idea of America being a "melting pot" is counter-productive and counterintuitive to the outcomes and goals it promotes. Melting in a boiling pot of racism, sexism, and xenophobia is a recipe for disaster. What is happening in America today results from its "melting pot" idea, anchored in social identity theory. Many people in the out-groups of whiteness are marginalized, discriminated against, and denied access to resources that would allow them to live up to the mantra of the Declaration of Independence – "We hold these truths to be self-evident, that all men are created equal, that they are endowed by their Creator with certain unalienable Rights, that among these are Life, Liberty and the pursuit of Happiness."[19] For some, the pursuit of happiness comes with severe conditions. Behaving and presenting oneself in a particular manner, even if it is outside of the cultural and ethnic norms one has been raised in and has associated with for years to be able to live and thrive in America.

Cognitive Development

Cognition involves the mental activities associated with thinking, remembering, knowing, and communicating. Schemas store the data collected during this cognitive process of active thinking. Schemas are concepts or mental molds into which we pour our experiences and memories.[20]

Schema theory provides a framework that helps organize and interpret past experiences and historical information in various environments. Schemas can effectively indicate in examining ergonomics (how people work in their environment) and how they make decisions. However, these mental frameworks can also cause the exclusion of pertinent information instead of focusing only on those factors that conform to our pre-existing beliefs and ideas. Schemas can contribute to stereotypes and make it difficult to retain new information that does not conform to our established ideas about the world.[21] This is why it is imperative for leaders to spend time with themselves to analyze and assess their behaviors and ideologies and discern through self-reflection where they come from. Stereotypes and biases are derivatives of history and memories.

According to Sigmund Freud (1856–1939), our levels of consciousness play an essential role in our behavior. Freud discussed the three levels of the mind as motives that lead to how we feel, act, and make decisions: the preconscious, conscious, and unconscious.[22] Our feelings, what motivates us, and our choices are not visible to anyone else. Yet, they are the most responsible for our behaviors. The unseen attributes significantly influence our past experiences in our unconscious mind. Therefore, we must spend time with ourselves to access and retrieve those memories and thoughts in our unconscious before a trigger drives them out.

Many psychologists and social psychologists suggest that unconscious biases develop early in childhood. Stimuli created from biological impulses and environmental influences can be stored away and forgotten. Retrieving and understanding as much of our unconscious being as we can is an essential process of SLIM.

The exercises in this workbook help reveal deeply rooted memories and experiences that hold unconscious ideas, thoughts, and experiences that may hinder constructing a realistic leadership identity.

Cognition helps reach these areas of the mind that are not readily accessible. Social psychologist Jean Piaget's Theory and Stages of Cognitive Development, include the concept of assimilation. Cognitive assimilation interprets new experiences from our current schemas (current understandings) as we interact with the world. We adjust or accommodate our schemas to incorporate information provided by new experiences. Too much assimilation and accommodation can distract us from becoming our ideal selves. So, it is crucial to understand your individualized framing to balance how you interact with others and the environment. This journal uses theory and methods that build that individualized framework.

The amount of time spent self-reflecting cannot be understated when examining our history and the leaders that shaped our society today, including abolitionists and other champions of freedom and individual rights. The *revolution* of your leadership identity recognizes the continuum of constant change and, hopefully, consistent understanding and growth in who we are. This change requires a systematic process to frequently "check ourselves" to ensure we are living up to the person we define for ourselves. Who we believe we are is probably the most underrated construct we spend the least time assessing and analyzing before determining and participating in that identity definition. The trailblazing first Black filmmaker, author, and producer of over 44 films, Oscar Micheaux (1884–1951), stated that our *"self-image is so powerful that it unwittingly becomes our destiny."*[23] Using a quote from a notable film producer may seem odd for a leadership identity book, but Micheaux is the perfect person to reference in this context. As the saying goes, life imitates art, or some may say art imitates life.

From either perspective, our lives are stories with a beginning, middle, and end. We don't have much control over how we get here and how we leave, but we can shape and define much of what is in the middle. Especially in our leadership roles, we tend to meld who we are with the expectations of others for us, and the latter often takes precedence.

Authenticity can be an interactive predictor of decision-making. A foundational concern with leadership today is the apparent lack of self-awareness and how historically and biologically normalized behaviors and practices perpetuate systemic educational, economic, social, and political inequality in this country that stifles life, liberty, and our pursuit of happiness. SLIM provides a tool for people to re-evaluate, re-position, and re-introduce their identities as leaders through the Schematic Leadership Identity Model (SLIM) framework.

Notes

1 Youssef, N. A., Lockwood, L., Su, S., Hao, G., & Rutten, B. P. F. (2018). The Effects of Trauma, with or without PTSD, on the Transgenerational DNA

Methylation Alterations in Human Offsprings. *Brain Sciences, 8*(5), 83. https://doi.org/10.3390/brainsci8050083

2   Davies, K. (2002). *Cracking the Genome: Inside the Race to Unlock Human DNA*. Johns Hopkins University Press.

3   Grand, S., & Salberg, J. (2017). *Trans-generational Trauma and the Other: Dialogues across History and Difference*. Routledge, Taylor & Francis Group.

4   Bushman, H. (2019). Large Study Reveals PTSD Has Strong Genetic Component like other Psychiatric Disorders. UC Health – UC San Diego. Retrieved November 29, 2022, from https://health.ucsd.edu/news/releases/Pages/2019-10-08-study-reveals-ptsd-has-strong-genetic-component.aspx

5   Jill Salberg and Sue Grand (eds), Wounds of History: Repair and Resilience in the Trans-generational Transmission of Trauma. *Psychoanalysis and History*, 20(2). Retrieved November 30, 2022, from https://euppublishing.com/doi/full/10.3366/pah.2018.0262

6   Leary, J. D., & Robinson, R. (2018). *Post Traumatic Slave Syndrome: America's Legacy of Enduring Injury and Healing*. Joy DeGruy Publications Inc.

7   Williams, T. M. (2009). *Black Pain: It Just Looks Like We're Not Hurting – Real Talk For When There's Nowhere To Go But Up*. Scribner.

8   Vinkers, C. H., Kalafateli, A. L., Rutten, B. P., Kas, M. J., Kaminsky, Z., Turner, J. D., & Boks, M. P. (2018). Traumatic Stress And Human DNA Methylation: A Critical Review. *Epigenomics*. Retrieved January 29, 2023, from https://pubmed.ncbi.nlm.nih.gov/26111031/

9   L'Ouverture, T., Aristide, J.-B., & Nesbitt, N. (2019). *The Haitian Revolution*. Verso.

10 Jawaid, A., Roszkowski, M., & Mansuy, I. M. (2018). Transgenerational Epigenetics of Traumatic Stress. *Progress in Molecular Biology and Translational Science*, 273–298. https://doi.org/10.1016/bs.pmbts.2018.03.003

11 Bargh, J. A. (2016). Awareness of the Prime Versus Awareness of its Influence: Implications for the Real-world Scope of Unconscious Higher Mental Processes. *Current Opinion in Psychology, 12*, 49–52. https://doi.org/10.1016/j.copsyc.2016.05.006

12 Bargh, J. A., & Morsella, E. (2008). The Unconscious Mind. *Perspectives on Psychological Science, 3*(1), 73–79. https://doi.org/10.1111/j.1745-6916.2008.00064.x

13 Starr, D. (2020). Meet the Psychologist Exploring Unconscious Bias – and its Tragic Consequences for Society. *Science*. Retrieved November 30, 2022, from https://www.science.org/content/article/meet-psychologist-exploring-unconscious-bias-and-its-tragic-consequences-society

14 Indian Removal Act: Primary Documents in American History: Introduction. *Research Guides*. (n.d.). Retrieved November 27, 2022, from https://guides.loc.gov/indian-removal-act

15 Cheney, A. (1994). *Lorraine Hansberry*. Twayne.

16 Margolis, J., May-Varas, S. & Mead, T. (eds) (2022). Social Cognitive Theory. *Educational Learning Theories*. 3rd edn https://openoregon.pressbooks.pub/educationallearningtheories3rd/chapter/chapter-3-social-cognitive-theory-2/

17 Howard, J. (2000). Social Psychology of Identities. *Annual Review of Sociology*. Retrieved February 8, 2023, from https://pdodds.w3.uvm.edu/files/papers/others/2000/howard2000.pdf

18 Hogg, M. A., & Abrams, D. (1990). *Social Identity Theory: Constructive and Critical Advances*. Harvester-Wheatsheaf.

19 National Archives and Records Administration. (n.d.). *Declaration of Independence: A Transcription*. National Archives and Records Administration. https://www.archives.gov/founding-docs/declaration-transcript

20 Rips, L. J. (2011). *Lines of Thought: Central Concepts in cognitive Psychology.* Oxford University Press.
21 Cherry, K. (2019, September 23). What Role Do Schemas Play in the Learning Process? *Verywell Mind.* Retrieved May 8, 2022, from https://www.verywellm ind.com/what-is-a-schema-2795873; Plant, K. L., & Stanton, N. A. (2012). The Explanatory Power of Schema Theory: Theoretical Foundations and Future Applications in Ergonomics. *Ergonomics, 56*(1), 1–15. https://doi.org/10.1080/ 00140139.2012.736542
22 Mcleod, Saul. (2023). Freud and the Unconscious Mind. *Simply Psychology.* https://www.simplypsychology.org/unconscious-mind.html
23 Reynolds, E. (2017). *Hidden African American Films.* Publici.ucimc.org. http://publici.ucimc.org/

Chapter 5

Phase III

The Evolution – The Process

This chapter discusses how the SLIM model takes an epistemological leadership approach to determine how historical "normalized" practices, perceptions, and experiences influence leadership. The goal is to develop an individualized approach to provide the framework to reflect, build, and formalize leadership identity. This chapter illustrates SLIM's signature identification tools: personal mission, vision, value proposition statements, Layers of the Mind–Mental habit, behavior, and value identifications, and the schematic model, which help in preparation for the self-guided journal entries and assessments that follow in the remaining chapters.

The Art and Science of Identity

The world is a place that is chaotic and unpredictable, even in its balanced natural patterns and cycles. Through the predictable patterns of the universe, humans have been able to identify seasons and navigate life despite nature's reign. These patterns in nature – symmetrical petals on a flower, the layered pines on a pinecone, and the waves of water in the ocean – give our world identity and our lives logic and order. The dichotomy of balance and chaos in nature is similar to the contrasts and complexities of our identities – layered with deliberate patterns and speckled with actions akin to unexplained wonders of the world.

Who we are is not a static concept. Identities change based on our experiences, history, and memories. Knowledge of self is a consequence of doing the work. When leaders take time to understand their identity and why they behave and think the way they do, they can constantly conflict with their environment. The normalization and expectations of those around you require you to be a certain way – all the time. Indeed, we have all experienced someone we know well who does something contrary to our expectations of who we think they are. We attribute this new behavior to something being "wrong" in their lives when sometimes people merely exercise their right to be all they are.

DOI: 10.4324/9781003394051-5

Business leaders, political figures, philanthropists, and social activists believe that one key to success is expanding and exploring one's identity. People constructing their identity in the way they believe serves them is the art of identity. Still, nature has a significant say in our biological and psychological makeup that may be difficult to remove from whom we think and say we are. As discussed earlier, that nature can be the generational pull in our genetic makeup. Arguably, the formulation of one's identity is patterns of our behaviors or habits that derive from a sense of convenience or repetition stemming from biological and psychological memories, experiences, and social factors.

This leadership framework positions leaders to unravel deeply rooted experiences and memories that may encourage behaviors and habits not conducive to reaching their aspirational selves.

SLIM uses self-guided examinations through journaling and assignments to frame an individual's journey through social cognition and internal and external analysis of histories and memories.

What is SLIM?

Social Cognition Assessment + Individualized Analysis + Leadership Assessments = Leadership Identity Schema

Schematic Leadership Identity Model (SLIM) is a Social Cognitive Self-Assessment designed to guide leaders on the seven-phase identity journey with two main phases – The Revolution (Phase I) and The Evolution phases (Phases III–VII).

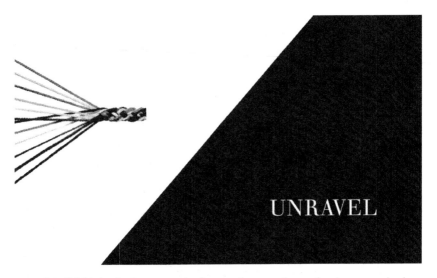

UNRAVEL

Figure 5.1 SLIM helps leaders recognize factors that constitute who they are as leaders.

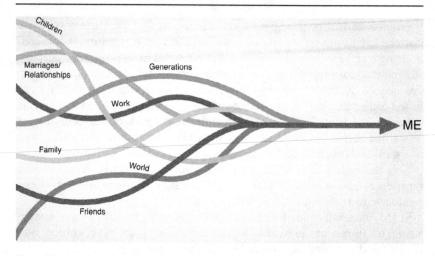

Figure 5.2 SLIM provides a tool that helps leaders unravel the details of each factor and determine if or how they want it as a part of their leadership identity.

The Revolutionary phase recognizes that personal change is necessary and begins the historical self-reflection essential in growth and development, and the Evolutionary phase is the continual process of self-discovery utilizing several assignments and journaling processes.

SLIM takes an epistemological leadership approach to truth, belief, and justification of one's leadership identity by examining leadership behaviors. Truth is an incident where there are no false propositions. One's truth is not facts; one's truth is one's experience. Belief is one's acceptance that something is true. Justification is the rationale of one's belief.

This method takes a historical approach to predict, describe, empower, and deconstruct views about decisions, behavior, habits, values, and ideologies. Unlike many leadership assessments, SLIM does not focus on a leader's abilities or skills, but the anchoring of this model is on a leader's choices and how and why they behave and think the way they do.

The SLIM framework considers psycho-historical and psychobiological variables that influence perspectives, attitudes, and behaviors that in turn influence decision-making. Psychohistory is the interpretation of an individual's historical events and psychological history. Psychobiology is the biological basis of behavior and thoughts.

In the broadest (and briefest) sense, a socio-historical study of leadership coalesces the aims, philosophies, and methodologies of historiography with those of the social and cultural sciences, meaning it analyzes the interpretation and practice of leadership through the lens of social/historical contexts, scientific discovery, and tradition. The result is a better understanding of the self's origin, development, and

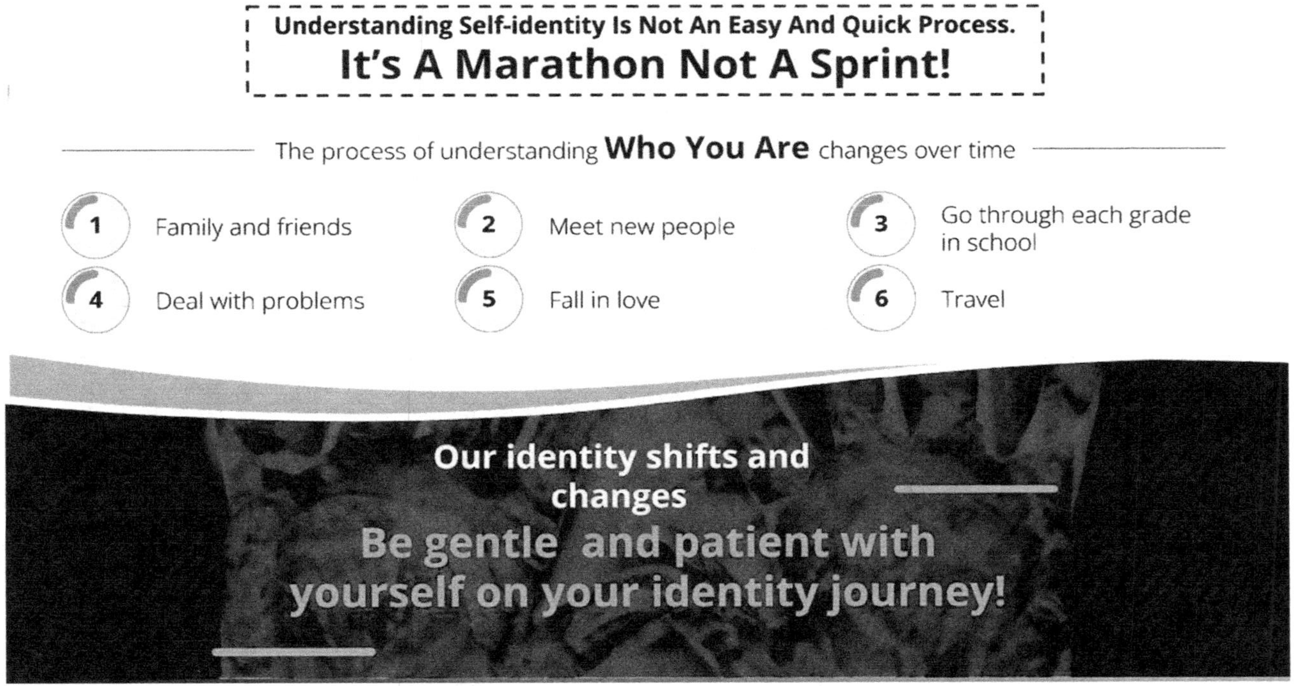

Understanding Self-identity Is Not An Easy And Quick Process.

It's A Marathon Not A Sprint!

The process of understanding **Who You Are** changes over time

1 Family and friends

2 Meet new people

3 Go through each grade in school

4 Deal with problems

5 Fall in love

6 Travel

Our identity shifts and changes

Be gentle and patient with yourself on your identity journey!

Figure 5.3 External factors that may shift one's leadership identity

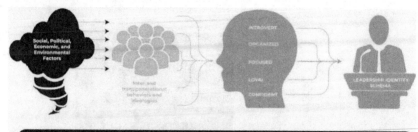

Figure 5.4 The SLIM Model

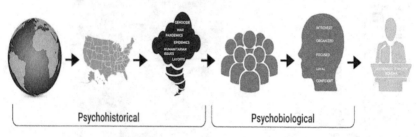

Figure 5.5 SLIM's external and internal theories that comprises the model

expression and how decisions are derived. The social history of leaders affects behaviors and decision-making. This clarification allows for the recognition of cultural and institutional influences in leadership.

SLIM provides a framework for self-reflection of:

a   History
b   Memory
c   Culture
d   Social & Professional Capital (trust, values, beliefs)

The second half of this book is a workbook with journal entries and assessments that allow leaders to reflect, build, and formalize their leadership identity.

Each evaluation and journal entry strengthens the evolution of the journey of self-discovery of identity that can lead to successful leadership outcomes. Each examination discovers the interconnectedness of memory and experiences that fuse the leaders' perspectives and knowledge that inform their leadership approaches. SLIM delivers a leadership model that is antithetical to many leadership assessment outcomes. This model presents a new approach to strengthening leadership capital through self-

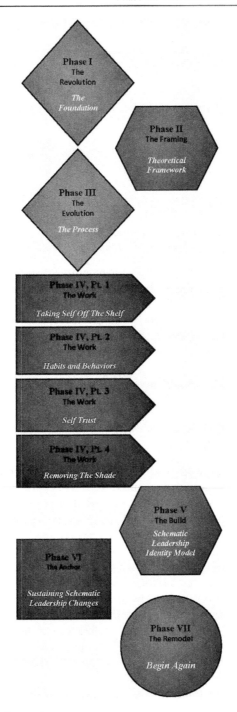

Figure 5.6 SLIM Framework

The **Evolution** is the continuous change that will happen in your identity journey as you grow and experience life

Figure 5.7 SLIM's Revolutionary and Evolutionary Phases

ideation. SLIM embraces history and memory's importance and impact on our daily behaviors, habits, beliefs, and values.

These exercises consider the socio-historical variables entrenched in the leader's perspective. Journal entries allow leaders to analyze behaviors, habits, values, and experiences that may not align with a leader's aspirations of whom they want to become. This model supports reflection, criticality, and theory to guide an approach to leadership that can produce success in personal and professional leadership roles.

Summary of SLIM

Leadership Identity Schema

A schema is a framework to organize and interpret information and a place where experiences are poured into concepts or mental molds. Psychologist, F.C. Bartlett (1932), offered that memories take the form of a schema providing a mental framework for remembering and understanding information. Bartlett's research and other research on reflective memory have found that in many cases recall and reinterpretation of memories and experiences are altered to simplify the story. Schemas in SLIM are designed to prevent leaders from excluding important information on how we define and see ourselves.

SLIM helps recognize behaviors that assimilate or accommodate an identity outside your constructed, referenced schema. Does either approach serve whom you want to become in your leadership identity journey? The leadership evolutionary journey requires distinguishing between habits, values, trust indicators, and characteristics. An essential factor is determining thoughts and behaviors – in the preconscious, conscious, and unconscious – to the identity schema to discern whether these

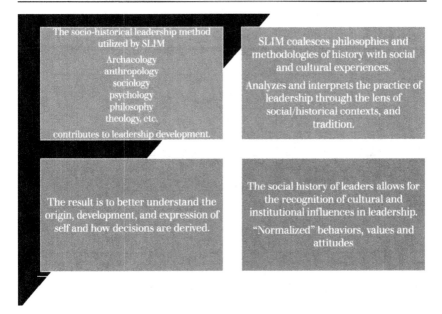

Figure 5.8 Summary of SLIM's objectives

factors need to be removed, modified, or kept in the identity framework. Practicing reflection opens the possibility of retrieving memories that explain behaviors. Consistency of this process helps uncover those unconscious habits and behaviors that influence important values, feelings, and motivations.

There has been significant research conducted on identity. Psychologists and social scientists have differing opinions about the phenomenon of behavior and identity. How, if at all, can identity be viewed and measured? Much of the research has been quantitative to reveal and explain characteristics and traits. But SLIM© is a qualitative self-assessment that supports a narrative introspection of one's ideation of self. This task is challenging and requires self-trust and honesty to see ourselves and recognize the areas we must pay close attention to or remove from our identity schema.

The Mind Matters Tables can offer organization in the identity evolution journey as you go through the journal exercises and assessments. Leaders should revisit these tables often as their identity schema shifts and changes.

Define Yourself for Yourself

Often a leader's mission and vision are the same as their organization's mission and vision. In addition, sometimes personal value propositions get lost when who they are is submerged in the company's ethos. Therefore, leaders take on the company's vision of who they want them to be as leaders.

Habits	Values, Feelings, Motivations	Behaviors (Responses)
Solitude in intial professional settings	Protective	Cautious, questioning
Decision-maker	Goal-oriented, feeling accomplished	embrace problems and constraints
Quick to make decisions	Anxiety	Inefficient goal setting
Little sleep	mental, emotional, and physical health	Quiet, irritable
Can be sharp and quick-witted	Do not like being disrespected/ undervalued	Defensive stance, protective

Figure 5.9 Preconscious Example

Habits	Values, Feelings, Motivations	Behaviors (Responses)
Networker	Build Relationships	Outgoing
Decision-maker	Self-confident	Multi-tasking, thorough
Organized	Clarity, Clean, Structured	Multi-tasking
Spend time with family and friends	Community	Loyal
Creative	First-mover, self-confidont	Seeking new ways to solve problems/ Embrance problems and constraints
Alone time	Spirituality	Meditation/prayer

Figure 5.10 Conscious Example

Habits	Values, Feelings, Motivations	Behaviors (Responses)
Small circle	Not trusting of people's motives	Not open or inviting to some people
Decision-maker	Controlling because others may not be capable	Multi-tasking, overworked
Setting expectations	Often disappointed in people	Internalize feelings until they can no longer be contained (blow-ups)
Alone time	Self-doubt	Meditation/prayer

Figure 5.11 Unconscious Example

Habits	Values, Feelings, Motivations	Behaviors (Responses)

Figure 5.12 Preconscious

Habits	Values, Feelings, Motivations	Behaviors (Responses)

Figure 5.13 Conscious

Habits	Values, Feelings, Motivations	Behaviors (Responses)

Figure 5.14 Unconscious

IDENTITY VALUE PROPOSITION, MISSION, AND VISION EXAMPLE

Your Identity Value Proposition (the clearest benefit (value) from being you)
Example: I am a community builder, loyalist, and innovator – I have a great sense of humor, I am creative, and a life-long learner.

Your Identity Mission (your raison d'etre – purpose – reason for being - intention)
Example: To use my creativity as a tool to educate and address social issues.

Your Identity Vision (who you aspire to be long term – your "be")
Example: Continue to seek the truth in self and others to make an impact in the world using my creative talents and knowledge to impact one life at a time.

Figure 5.15 SLIM's Identity Value Proposition, Mission and Vision Example

IDENTITY VALUE PROPOSITION, MISSION, AND VISION

Your Identity Value Proposition (the clearest benefit (value) from being you)
_____
_____
_____

Your Identity Mission (your raison d'etre – purpose – reason for being - intention)
_____
_____
_____

Your Identity Vision (who you aspire to be long term – your "be")
_____
_____
_____

Figure 5.16 SLIM's Identity Value Proposition, Mission and Vision Exercise

Leaders tend to move further away from their authentic, natural selves. This alignment, in turn, does not give them the space to understand the ebbs and flows their experiences have on their identities. Too often, leaders align who they are with the job description and expectations that the role requires, hopefully leading to leadership success. The problem becomes losing oneself in a position. Now, this in no way suggests that a leader should not meet the needs of their job responsibilities. This framework offers a way for them to do that without altering their natural progression of who they want to be and their desired selves. By taking time to frame your identity based on your values and goals, you could be more effective as a leader and align more with your aspirational self.

As you evolve in your journey, discern your Identity Value Proposition, design your mission and vision beyond what you do, and anchor it in whom you desire to be. Remember, our identity is not static, so we should constantly revisit, re-evaluate, redefine, and reposition who we are.

Figure 5.18 Identity value proposition, mission, and vision

Chapter 6

Phase IV, Part I
The Work – Taking Self Off the Shelf

At what age do we begin to identify with self?
When does the concept of self begin?
What things, actions, or people help guide us along the way?
Are we predisposed to our identity in the womb?

As Frederick Douglass (1852) indicated in his eloquent address *What to the Slave Is the Fourth of July*, "We have to do with the past only as we can make it useful to the present and the future."[1] The focus on history and memories is not to take a stroll down memory lane or relish what has happened. As Douglass urged, knowledge of the past is a formidable tool for positioning ourselves for the future. This tool can only be effective if the information effects change. There is no forward movement and progress without shifting. Looking back strengthens our ability to be successful in the future. Regarding identity, it is often necessary to go back as far as possible to understand the nuances of self.

The American Psychoanalytic Association suggests that identifying oneself begins as early as 18 months.[2] Beginning in preschool, cooperative play, which focuses on children solving problems by working together to achieve a common goal, gives children an early start on the principles of teamwork. But can this become too manipulative, which results in behavior that is the opposite of whom the child would have eventually self-identified? Ironically, soon after a child recognizes their identity, they are made to store it away on the shelf like building blocks or crayons to be retrieved later. In many American schools, the development process could be more conducive to deliberate consciousness of self. It may be fear of an exaggerated perception of self or merely to satisfy the instructional need of the classroom for collaboration and cooperation. We often consider ego a negative character trait when it can be healthy and revered if channelled constructively. Recognizing the self requires merely a reflection. But, developing an identity is crafted, either honestly or to an end. Does how and what we teach our children early change the conscious thought of their identity? Does the educational system teach our children to think independently, which is a derivative of who they are, or does the system require children to adapt to a pre-defined self of what society says they should be?

DOI: 10.4324/9781003394051-6

illustrated by Jada E Harris

Figure 6.1 Is your identity stored away on the shelf like a rag doll or an old book collecting dust?

How we learn and the diverse nature of how our conscious thoughts receive, and process information impact our attitudes and behaviors. This knowledge is valuable to understanding who we are in our identity process. Early self-awareness could prevent later behaviors such as bullying, depression, low self-esteem, and other issues.[3] Collaboration and self-awareness do not need to be mutually exclusive.

Suppose we championed self-identity and individualism as much as we collaborate, or at least have a balanced approach. This practice could strengthen team outcomes by allowing individuals to have the confidence to show up as themselves and bring with them their creativity and innovation. Let's retrieve the building blocks of our identity that lock in our memories and hidden traits.

Consider beginning the identity journey by considering our behaviors, values, and habits as nutrients and supplements. According to the World Health Organization, a nutrient is a substance the body requires for survival and growth.[4] The best way to receive nutrients is by naturally consuming food. But, if the foods are not providing adequate nourishment, many people turn to supplements to get the daily requirement or additional nutrients. When nutrients are deficient, external sources are added to the diet to increase what is naturally lacking – vitamins and other needed iron and minerals. When someone believes they are not who they want to be (or the self is deficient – self-confidence, self-awareness, and self-identity), behaviors, attitudes, and values may be added or modified to meet the expectations of the idealized self or the version of themselves expected of them from others.

What behaviors, values, and habits come naturally, which may be derived from outside influences to supplement the person you need or want to be? For those that come naturally, when did they start? Why did they start? How did they start?

The first two journal entries will help unravel some behaviors, habits, values, and ideologies that have been there since childhood. Do not worry if specific behaviors or values are not apparent during these first few entries. Things may not come the first time through the process, it may take several times in this evolutionary process to retrieve the details you need to build your identity schema. Remember to give yourself grace throughout this journey.

JOURNAL EXERCISE I

Who we are today often reflects our past experiences and memories. How we grew up, our experiences at school and home, our friends, the joys, and the trauma we have experienced reflect who we are today. *Taking Self Off The Shelf* is reflecting on the source of certain behaviors, values, and attitudes to determine if they result from our natural Self or a consequence of social identity influences. Then, either keep, modify, or remove these things from your identity schema. In this exercise, take time to reflect on your earliest memories. Dig deep. Consider why you have that memory, what was happening in your environment, and how that memory represents (or does not) or reflects who you are today. Try to tell the whole story and do not leave out unflattering or perhaps confusing parts. This information could be essential to unraveling your identity. Begin with one memory and build on that memory until the culmination of memories begins to form a story about your past and how it informs your present.

Memory Entries:

Notes

1 Aggarwal-Schifellite, M. (2020, June 30). Reading to Explore the Resonance of Douglass' Famous Speech. *The Harvard Gazette.* https://news.harvard.edu/gazette/story/2020/06/reading-to-explore-the-resonance-of-douglass-famous-speech/
2 Mcleod, S. (2023, May 1). Erik Erikson's Stages of Psychosocial Development. *Simply Psychology.* https://www.simplypsychology.org/Erik-Erikson.html
3 Mcleod, S. (2023, May 1). Erik Erikson's Stages of Psychosocial Development. *Simply Psychology.* https://www.simplypsychology.org/Erik-Erikson.html
4 Nutrients 101 – What Are Nutrients Anyway?. *Health Start Foundation* (n.d.). https://www.healthstartfoundation.org/hsblog/what-are-nutrients-anyway#

Chapter 7

Phase IV, Part 2
The Work – Habits and Behaviors

Our history, memories, and past experiences are formative to our identities. Yet, it is essential to remember that as we recall our history, we don't have to rehearse it to the point of performance. Suppose we continue to re-enact our past experiences through our habits and behaviors intentionally. In that case, it will influence our future in much the same way. To know and understand our history is not to mimic it but to use it as a foundation to re-evaluate, reassess, and reposition our identity. If we don't know and understand our history, there is no anchoring for change and transformation that we all need to be better people.

Liberation needs confrontation. Confronting our past is vital to understanding our identity and having the freedom to define ourselves. This knowledge liberates us from habits, behaviors, thoughts, and beliefs that no longer serve who we strive to be as leaders and human beings. The benefit of self-liberation is multifaceted because the rewards go beyond individual achievement. Unlocking your identity and freeing yourself from ideas and beliefs that have defined who you were in the past also benefits your ecosystem (family, workplace, community). Imitation and fabrication of identity could lead to habits and behaviors that trick the mind into believing it is one's natural self.

The mind is a highly complex organ that retains information that can unlock many of our problems and unanswered questions about ourselves. Retrieving these answers requires work. The reward for our actions is knowledge, whether positive or negative experiences. There are lessons in every outcome. Continue this journey with an understanding that we all have things we need to work on to be better tomorrow than we were today. Traditions are not our trademarks. We have a choice what behaviors, attitudes, and values we bring forth from our past and assign to our identity.

Habits, Goals, Behaviors, and Values...Oh My!

In the past few years, world scientists and historians have cemented the importance of human beings recognizing the patterns in the world. As

DOI: 10.4324/9781003394051-7

discussed earlier in the book, understanding seasons was one of the most critical phenomena humans identified. Understanding the weather patterns helped construct roles, communities, and family dynamics because it set a standard of living throughout the year based on the weather. Today, our habits and behaviors disclose patterns in our identity that indicate our professional and personal positions and how we situate ourselves in these ecosystems.

Habit-Identity Theory

Habits can be good indicators of self-identity. Many of our behaviors are habitual – getting up at a particular time, brushing our teeth, showering, making coffee, getting dressed, and leaving for work. Many people have other habitual behaviors, including the times to eat daily, when and where they work out, and on which days they dine out and socialize. Even at work, our moves can be predictable. Habits also involve other people – our teams, organizations, and families.

How one sees oneself – self-actualization – is manifested through one's memories, beliefs, motivations, recurrent thoughts, emotions, and self-perceptions, which are constantly reconstructed and revised. But this representation also reveals itself in habits. Families, friends, and environment also play critical roles in dictating to us who we are. Sigmund Freud's theory of psychoanalytic behaviors in psychology explores how our unconscious mind and childhood experiences affect our behavior. Many psychological processes, specifically socio-cognitive processes, work to help create our self-identities. Habits develop from personal decision-making. Studies have found that when habits align with identity, the outcome is often seeking an ideal self, cognitive self-integration strengthens, and self-esteem increases. Strong motivations to uphold a specific identity may instigate repeated actions or behaviors, especially those habits that result from assimilation and code-switching, which is changing our behaviors (how we dress, how we speak, and our actions) to conform to an environment or culture that is different from our native environment or culture. Habits form because they relieve people from thinking or processing information. Many believe habits are essential to our essence and identity and are often challenging to break. But when people do the work to understand why they behave in ways contrary to who they want to be, those habits can be shifted or removed. Schematic identity habits are habits, behaviors, and actions attached to goals and values affirmed.

Habits and Values

Habits range from small, unimportant actions to large and complex behaviors, such as tying your shoes, how you travel to work, or when you cook or eat dinner. Some habits link directly to our values, like donating to a specific charity or exercising.

Questions exist about whether, how, or when habits contribute to our identity. If habits contribute to identity, how do beliefs about self, such as self-esteem and self-regulation, embed into our psyche and impact who we are?

Self-ideations are mental representations that individuals hold about themselves, including autobiographical memories, self-attributions, beliefs, motivations, recurrent thoughts, emotions, and self-perceptions. Construction and revision of these narratives happen often.[1]

Habits may become part of self-identities through various psychological processes. As socio-cognitive models suggest, one such method may result from enacted motivations.

A strong motivation anchored in self-identity may instigate repeated action, becoming a habit. Such habits function as vehicles of self-control in accomplishing a plan or dream. Habits relieve an individual from having to deliberate and decide on actions and may thus promote achieving a goal.[2] Another path to a habit-identity relationship is through self-perception. Through the perception of our frequently performed behaviors, we may infer that these are important to us and may thus be part of who we are.[3]

Habits often serve an individual value or goal. Studies have found that habits help identify who we are when considering goals and values. When habits relate to feelings of identity, this comes with stronger cognitive self-integration, higher self-esteem, and a striving toward an ideal self.[4].

Developing and rebuilding a leadership identity schema may require habits and behaviors to change, which requires seeing and believing new things about yourself. Your past self cannot be erased, but you can use experiences to formulate new habits and behaviors, culminating in your ideal leadership identity.

There is nuance in habits and behaviors. These two things are not the same. Habits are practices and things people repeatedly do until those things become natural and innate. Behaviors are reactionary actions taken in response to something or someone, even oneself. Behaviors can be involuntary or voluntary, whereas habits are performed automatically without thought or contemplation. There is also a difference between behaviors and identity. Behavior does not define who you are. If you exhibit toxic behaviors, that does not necessarily make you toxic.

Identity Behavioral Theory

Developing a concept of self and self-identity comes with the development of moral identification. From an early age, we learn right from wrong and what behaviors dictate these socially constructed misnomers. Repeating such moral behaviors may become moral habits and feed a moral identity. Such habits may then result in character traits or dispositions.[5]

The second view of the relationship between habit and identity is a philosophical examination developed by Wagner and Northoff (2014).

These authors present the difference between "personhood" and "personal identity." Personhood defines the components of a person at one specific point in time. These features are fluid and not permanent; thus, to present as the same person, details must remain stable to have a personal identity. Wagner and Northoff (2014) considered habit as an explanatory construct that links these different temporal dimensions to form a unique identity.[6]

There are significant associations between habits and self-identity that reach beyond psychology. Still, studies need to be more consistent with how extensive the correlation between habits and identity is. There is a considerable variation between studies in the scope of habit-identity correlations.

This difference suggests that only certain habits are related to self-identity. Studies indicate that identity-related habits are attached to a person's goals or values. Goals and values may be associated with one's self-concept and are likely to be repeatedly practiced.[7]

In summary, behaviors become part of self-identity in two cases:

1   If the behavior is repeated and automatic it becomes a habit ingrained in the person's autobiographical memory.
2   If the behavior is related to an important goal or value.

Perception and memory play an essential role in assessing habits and behaviors. Practicing behaviors and habits that may not align with your socialized ideation of self or your acceptance of how others see you may be challenging. The journaling and assignments in upcoming chapters will be critically important to your self-discovery evolution and defining your leadership schema.

Sustainability of Habits and Behaviors

The longevity of a behavioral change associated with identity requires behaviors maintained over time. There are many questions to work through on your identity journey. Decisions include whether behaviors should become habits to sustain self-identity or if they should be modified or removed. This workbook provides a framework to analyze and explore behavioral changes. This model recognizes what new behaviors align with self-ideation, and which would be beneficial as a habit in one's schematic identity model. Thorough reflection can help free those repressed, unconscious memories and thoughts manifested in habits, behaviors, attitudes, values, and beliefs.

Summary

Habits should be distinguished from behaviors, especially when determining one's identity. Behaviors are responses, impulses, or actions to your environment and the people in your environment. Habits are repetitive things that a person does that become second nature. Habits are internally focused, while behaviors are externally focused. Some habits serve a self-identifying purpose, mainly when considered in the context of goals or values. Our behaviors can result from our experiences and memories that form habits when done repeatedly and automatically. A strong motivation anchored in self-identity may instigate repeated actions and behaviors becoming habits. Such habits may function as vehicles of self-control in accomplishing a goal. Habits relieve an individual from having to deliberate and decide on actions and may thus promote the accomplishment of a plan.[8]

Reflection

Many research studies have theorized that the conversion of experience creates knowledge. SLIM takes a holistic approach to evaluating self-development. The experience is central to analyzing what we know about ourselves and how we learn, develop, and grow. Self-reflection is impossible without past experiences. Reflection forms concepts that drive how we see the world and our environment and ultimately influence our behaviors.

David Kolb's Experiential Learning Theory (ELT) is a theoretical model that guides navigating and uncovering personal and social ideologies that underpin leadership decisions.[9] Like Social Learning Theory and others, ELT examines how learners interact with their environment to create new knowledge.[10] Experience is central to changed behavior, but only as much as the experience is explored and contemplated. Leadership identity strategies that present a means for leaders to conduct reflective analysis of their experiences (memories and history) can support the vision of a new or updated identity model and evaluate the efficacy of a leader's behaviors and habits. These leadership models will arguably result in more effective and sustainable leadership behaviors than those focusing on surfaced leadership traits and characteristics.

Differentiating cognitive and behavioral approaches to leadership development that focus on mental processing does not diminish the role of subjective experiential learning. Cognitive models explore the mental processes (levels of consciousness), behavioral models deal with the impact of the environment on external behaviors, and experiential learning delves into internal changes that occur during the reflection process of those experiences. SLIM combines all three philosophies in a focused reflection that examines complex and, at times, problematic behaviors, habits, and ideologies manifested from past experiences. This review helps reveal the source of behaviors driven by ideologies, values, and DNA transference as denoted by current research. These extractions of embedded memories can retrieve areas of ourselves that we do not necessarily recognize and identify those things that need strengthening.

SLIM seeks to reveal leadership identity beyond the descriptive analysis of leadership behavior. This model allows leaders to examine their history to uncover the meaning behind the behaviors, attitudes, and ideologies that were established.

My Behavioral Reflection

Many things may trigger the reflective journaling process. Sometimes it may be a memory that triggers it, thinking about the future, or a scheduled time allocated for writing and reflection. These behavioral reflections that I share were triggered thoughts during a time of grief after the loss of my parents 12 days apart in August 2018 and the loss of my brother just a few months later.

When my parents passed away, I wanted to unravel my life to the extent that I remembered every conversation, laugh, and cry I experienced with them. Going through pictures and keep-sakes, I began by reflecting on my school years. While reviewing my early school papers, I realized some consistencies with my primary teachers' comments about me. My teachers noted how bashful I was in class from kindergarten to sixth grade. Then in middle school, I no longer received those comments from my teachers. These progress reports unlocked some necessary information about my identity growth and framework.

I recall my being to myself at school in my early primary years, but I also like to be alone at home. I would not consider myself an introvert. I was very interested in what was happening in my environment, but I took caution with my words and actions. I was picked on in middle school for being tall, thin, and dark-skinned, but I ignored the taunting and the people who participated. That does not mean that the comments and jokes did not hurt my feelings because they did. But my mode of operation for handling conflict was to ignore it.

In the summer of 1981, I was a rising 9th grader. I stood head and shoulders above most students, so it was unsurprising that the basketball coach, Mr. Smart, was interested in my playing. After that first practice, the game had my heart. Mr. Smart was a very kind and encouraging coach. He made his players want to play and do their best, which is critical when working with young athletes. I had a natural athleticism on the court, and the following year, I focused on the fundamentals of the game. After the tremendous showing in my 9th grade first game, I was moved up to the varsity team the following year. This move meant I would have a different coach.

The varsity coach's personality was the antithesis of Mr. Smart. The varsity coach was aggressive, both verbally and physically. He would yell and throw balls in practice, mainly at me. Our characters were like oil and water, but he knew the team needed me. When we won games, it was a team effort. When we lost, somehow, it was my inability to perform or my lack of effort. I was one of two or three Black players on the basketball team for most of my high school career. The coach's behavior made it obvious to pinpoint his favorite players and those who were not. I did not have an issue with him playing favoritism as much as I had a problem with the blatant disrespect he constantly showed me. I initially believed he treated me horribly because he wanted me to be my best, so I never said anything. But as I continued to keep my feelings bottled up, I realized that it was only a matter of time before that bottle exploded. In my senior year, I would take direction from the assistant coach in practice to avoid confrontation with the coach. I never responded to his verbal and physical taunts and abuse until the last tournament game of my high school career.

My mother and brother had attended all my games since eighth grade, so it was unsurprising when they drove a few hours for this state tournament. I played every position in my senior year, but for this game I played the center position. In my senior year, I was 5'9, short for a center. Throughout the tournament, the girls I defended were often much taller and had more girth and muscle. At the final game, I had to guard a girl who was 6'3 and a fantastic all-around player. We lost badly, which was unusual for our team. After the game, the coach was in the locker room on one of his tirades about me, and I had had enough. So, I stood up for myself and told him basketball was a team sport, so he should not blame me for all our losses. I remember he walked across the room and stood inches away from me. He placed his hand around my neck and raised me from the ground to push me against the lockers. He told me to never speak to him that way again. Before my feet hit the floor, one of my teammates ran to get my mother and brother. Even though my brother is twelve years older than me, we have always been close. He and my mother never missed a game, so they witnessed many of my coach's tirades.

My brother handled the situation as most brothers would – physically, grabbing the coach in the same way he had grabbed me. I remember being scared because several school security officers had to separate my brother from my coach. Once hearing what happened in the locker room, I recall one of the officers saying the coach was lucky my brother did not throw down the stairs. The assistant coaches were also disgusted by the coach's actions, and they both checked on me to ensure I was physically and emotionally okay. Physically I was okay; emotionally, not so much. How does a 17-year-old young girl handle this trauma? Even though I knew I had done nothing to deserve what the coach had done, for a moment, I believe I thought it was my fault for responding to him in the locker room. Thankfully, my mother, brother, and the principal reassured me that I had done nothing wrong, but there was no undoing the emotional and mental harm this incident had caused. I know this affected my ability to trust those outside of my family.

A critical lesson from this experience is how my mother handled the situation. My mother showcased her ability to balance being a Black mother with the freedom to speak her mind. The ability to speak freely and experience the fullness of expression was, and still is, challenging for Black women to navigate due to the repercussion of being labeled an "angry Black woman." I always admired how comfortable she was in her skin and how she did not get caught up in stereotypes and characterizations historically established about who we are.

Everyone who knew my mother – friends in the neighborhood, family, colleagues at work, or teachers and administrators at the school – knew she was fiercely protective of her children and husband. So, while we sat in the principal's office, I recall the principal asking my mother how she wanted the situation handled. She did not raise her voice; she was emphatic about removing this coach from coaching girls' sports due to his inability to respect young girls. The principal obliged my mother's wishes and fired the coach that day. Interestingly, some teammates never spoke to me again, blaming me for the coach's dismissal. Although they never talked to me about it, I am sure some felt I should not have said anything to him. Most of the team stood beside me, knowing first-hand how physically and verbally abusive the coach was towards me.

His malice towards me did not stop after his firing. During the college recruitment process, the coach refused to release my tapes to colleges that were interested in me. I remember going to the coach's office with the list of colleges that I was interested in and who had requested my tapes. The coach looked at the list and asked, "Why do you want to attend these weird colleges? The list was Historically Black Colleges and Universities (HBCUs). My best friend at the time was a student at the University of Cincinnati. She helped me write a letter to the school to release the basketball tapes to college coaches so we could send them out ourselves. This basketball experience was a horrible way to end my high school career. I decided not to play basketball in college, although several universities recruited me. After reflecting on these memories, I cannot help but wonder if my not playing in college had something to do with the situation, I encountered with the HS coach. My last year of playing high school basketball heightened my awareness of race and racism and how arbitrary it often is.

Behavior Reflection Takeaway: Do not allow things to fester. Strengthen communication practices regarding addressing problematic situations. Quiet and observant – not bashful and introverted, as described by others. The anchoring of this behavior is unknown, but there are earlier memories of being quiet and insular at home with family. The large family dynamics may be key to further unlocking knowledge about these behaviors.

This basketball reflection and its takeaways brought me to an incident when I worked in corporate America in the information technology industry. I also experienced hurtful incidents that ignited my desire to speak and not be quiet. There are so many incidents, unfortunately, that I have journaled about, but I will only share a few in this book. The first incident was when I worked for a major insurance company in Ohio. This position was my first job after leaving Bowling Green State University. I worked for an older white woman. Like my basketball coach, this woman did not try to hide that she did not like me. All new hires had a coding partner to mentor them until their one-year probationary period ended. My coding partner asked me what I did to this woman because she told her I would not make it to a year. I asked my coding partner if it was my work, and she said I was doing great, which my quarterly performance evaluation also indicated. The incident that was insulting and traumatizing was when she refuted my having a miscarriage. After staying silent and focusing on my work, I could no longer allow her to disrespect my character, so I filed a formal complaint. She was in a leadership position but was certainly no leader. My only regret was never telling her how harmful her actions were. I felt like I was weak and partially responsible for her treating me disrespectfully because I never communicated my discomfort with her comments and actions. Ironically, I did make it to my 1st anniversary, and the company offered me a permanent position. After a few months, I resigned to move to Atlanta.

Behavior Reflection Takeaway: Be willing to stand by your principles and do not ignore those gut feelings, which are unconscious cognitive thoughts. The journaling and reflective process help explore and navigate your cognition, which brings awareness to ideas already in your consciousness. To stand by your principles, you must know what they are. Establishing boundaries will help frame your identity. Honor yourself, trust yourself, and trust what your consciousness tells you about situations and people. It may be challenging in professional settings to put your values and principles first, but there are ways to do that and maintain the ethos of your organization. Build on this behavior (aligning with your principles) to strengthen your leadership identity.

After leaving the insurance company, I moved to Atlanta and started a position at a state agency as a computer programmer. My direct report was an interesting older man. Everyone thought he was mean, regardless of a person's race or creed, he did not like anyone seemingly. Everyone would yell and argue with this man, but I did not want to get into office politics or gossip, so I stayed to myself and focused on my work. After being there for a few years, we established a good rapport. I had received two promotions, and he often commented on my work ethic. He would also call me "Slim," which was totally unprofessional and made me cringe, but there was no correcting him. I had already reported my previous manager to HR in my previous position, so I wanted to try to handle this on my own. When I got engaged, he was excited for me, and he and his wife gave us a beautiful vase as a wedding gift. People around the office found it strange that we genuinely worked well together. A year after I married, I put in my resignation. I remember he called me into his cubicle. He began to tell me about his life. He spoke of his father and how he grew up here in Atlanta when "white and Black just did not mix," he said. He told me his father raised him that way as a member of the Klu Klux Klan. He told me I was the only Black person he had ever loved. Wait, did this man say he loved me? Yes, he did. This cantankerous, mean, old white man raised to hate Black people realized, only after 70 years, that Blackness is not the caricatures dreamed up by white supremacists. As weird as this experience was, it is probably the most significant for me in terms of dealing with white people and racism.

Many Black people try to "teach" white folk how to not be racist by explaining how their actions and behaviors exemplify racism. Thousands of books also give this lesson. This experience showed me that people would derive their idealized selves when ready. Personal development work does not manifest outwardly until a level of the work is done. We can express for eternity that we have changed, but the proof reflects the internal work one invests in to produce new behavior, attitudes, and habits. I learned that showing up uniquely to you and truthfully can demand change from the people in your environment.

Behavior Reflection Takeaway: Do not change who you are and adjust your behavior for the sake of those in your environment. Establish a personal mission and vision and align that with your organization's mission and vision. These goals should influence your behavior. Steer away from those social influences, which can be significant. A leader needs to understand the implications of groupthink and trust themselves when making decisions. Being authentic may unlock barriers for others, but more significantly, your uniqueness will create opportunities for you.

When I left the state agency, I went to work for a software company. Initially hired as a computer programmer, I was quickly promoted to database administrator. For the first time in my professional career, I had a Black woman in a leadership role, Associate Vice President, to be exact. This role was my third corporate position, and my confidence in my work had grown significantly. I reported to a Black man who constantly demeaned and disrespected me, and one day I let him know that regardless of his title, I would not allow him to disrespect me without my addressing it. I challenged him every time I felt disrespected. He wrote me up, and the AVP wanted a word with me in her office. I respected this woman a lot. She showed up as herself and made no excuses for doing so. She was short, wore a close-cut natural afro, and had the loudest laugh that echoed throughout the office. Understand, this was the early 1990s when corporations had strict dress codes and certainly had an unwritten standard for hair (for Black folk in particular). Beyond her appearance, she was intelligent and a great leader. When I went into her office, she burst into laughter. She then shook her head and advised me on something I still carry. She suggested I always work hard and continue to have a great work ethic because my mouth would get me in trouble. But she told me not to silence my voice and to pick my battles. How poignant this advice was to hear. My full-circle moment.

Behavior Reflection Takeaway: Pick your battles. Not allowing circumstances and people to remove you from your identity framing is essential. Although situations may warrant attention, discern whether you are the one to address them and if it is worth the time and energy. Strengthen your critical thinking and protect your peace.

Years later, I worked for a company based in Europe, and many of its employees who worked in the Atlanta office were European. I managed a global team of database administrators. One of the project managers, an older white woman from Europe, always wanted my team to work over the weekend, giving very little notice. In this instance, I told her my group would not work over the weekend again because she could not correctly plan as a project manager. In the conference room at this meeting was the CIO, to whom we both reported, and a few of her colleagues. When the CIO agreed that my team should not work over the weekend, she became belligerent and pushed a chair across the conference room toward me. In shock, I looked at the CIO to intervene. He said nothing as she began to shout expletives at me. At this point, the human resource director, whose office was next to the conference room, ran into the room. She witnessed the woman cursing me and asked me to leave the conference room with her. I did. I was in my office for an hour fuming. I could not believe what had happened. After an hour, the CIO told me I had handled the situation well. He said I dealt with the incident well because I had not said anything. I suggested that had I pushed a chair toward this woman and cursed her the way she did me, I would have likely been escorted out of the building by police with possible assault charges pending. He assured me that would not have been the case, but I had experienced too much in that office to believe otherwise. Even still, I expected someone to do something. That never happened. I tried to excuse the woman's behavior away as stress and the pressure she was under, but this woman's unprofessional behavior did not stop. So, I filed a complaint with human resources as I had done with my first employer. Unlike the first complaint I filed, I remained at this company for many years and witnessed how this can change the dynamics of working relationships.

The breaking point in this role was when my direct report flew in to do my performance evaluation. I reported to the director of IT, and he told me that my work was good, and the customers had great things to say about my team's performance. He stated that they would give me more money but would not give me a promotion. At this moment, I knew I no longer wanted to work in a corporate environment. That year I left my position and began my academic and creative journeys.

I felt the pressure of being the only Black woman in the office and one of two Black women in this global company's leadership role. I was mindful of this fact, but the stress and pressure became overwhelming because, having found my voice, I could no longer sit quietly and not speak up and speak out against situations and behavior that were the antithesis of my values. I no longer wanted to carry the burden of being the "only one" – in the room, the team, and the company. Maybe I did not know how to code-switch or balance the need to assimilate into this corporate culture.

Interestingly, I was labeled a troublemaker because I needed to stand up for myself, reminiscent of my high school basketball experience. I was trying to figure out this woman and senior management, scouring conversations for their intentions, just as I did with my basketball coach. The culmination of these reflections has given me so much context regarding my behavior and attitude. My reflective journaling helped identify two things that have been barriers for me in progressing to my aspirational self – intentions, and expectations of others. Having put some time into my identity evolution, I realize that I spend too much time analyzing people's intentions, and I set expectations for people that they often cannot live up to. I excused behaviors for too long, seeking to evaluate people's hearts. What I know now is that the way that people treat you is their heart – at that time. The only way to tell if someone is on a personal development journey is through their actions and behavior. Because I am loyal, I stayed in relationships (professional and personal) too long. I sought people's intentions when their actions told me who they were all along. I also expected people to do things that I would do and how I would do them. One memory that gave an exception to this was the experience with the manager who opened up to me about his father being in the KKK. I had no expectations of him and did not spend time searching for why he was mean. His identity aligned with his behavior, and my behavior indicated who I was.

Behavior Reflection Takeaway: Restraint is not a weakness. Understand that it is not necessary to match someone else's crazy. Being still, observing, and taking notes will work out in your favor. Stop setting expectations of others and do not waste time trying to figure out people's intention when their actions and behavior tells you all you need to know.

A Note about the Journaling Process

I started journaling after my parents passed away because I believed my memories would keep me close to them. I did not realize how much my identity aligned with my parents and who they wanted me to be. Reflecting on these incidents brought awareness to my contemplation amid confrontation. I realized that, as I believed in high school, my silence was punishment for those who attacked me or wished me harm. I then felt disappointed in myself because I thought my silence was allowing people to continue disrespecting me.

I made it a point to write down the race and age of the people involved in these incidents because I was keenly aware of the historical implications of these behaviors. My being Black was central to these situations, even with the Black male manager. He did not disrespect my colleagues, who were white, and he certainly did not speak to the white women on our team in the manner he spoke to me. His behavior also has an anchoring in this country's history. Some Black people in a position of power feel as though they cannot support other Black people due to not wanting to be accused of showing favoritism or the fear of another Black person taking their spot. This lack of support often results in them treating their Black colleagues disrespectfully and in a discriminatory manner.

I can recall many more incidents, most of which involved white men and women. I cannot ignore this fact. What stood out in these reflections that I have been unable to unravel is their visceral disdain and behaviors toward me – my HS basketball coach, my first corporate supervisor, the project manager, and so on. Then there was the outlier, the grumpy older man, and the infamous son of a KKK who declared his platonic affection towards me. In her dissertation research titled, "The Criticality of Mentorship on the Trajectory of Imminent Black Female Leaders: A Phenomenological Narrative Inquiry," Dr. Jeanette Vaughn describes the importance of "reverse mentorship," whereby the mentee at some stage becomes the mentor providing a reciprocal learning experience in the relationship. This reciprocity is what unfolded in my experience with this man. He mentored me professionally as a computer programmer, and through my actions and behavior, I gave him the experience of getting to know a Black woman. He was at a point in his life where he was open to receiving, and that, in turn, possibly, aided him in even slightly altering his ideologies about who he thought I was to take in the fullness of who I was at that time.

When I fully embraced who I was, I felt better about myself, even if the outcome was not positive. I behaved with intention in high school because it came from an honest place. I was not privy to identity and the ebbs and flows of what that means. My behavior modeled my upbringing during these early stages of developing my identity schema. Dealing with my first supervisor, who accused me of lying about my miscarriage, was traumatizing. I was scared to lose my first job, so I allowed her to continuously disrespect me until I could no longer withstand her attacks. This experience almost destroyed my confidence in my work and had me questioning everything about myself – what I wore, how I spoke, how I walked, who I went to lunch with, etc. I look back on that incident now, feeling sorry for her and how miserable her life must have been.

Stitched in the fabric of this country are discriminatory and racist laws, and it is naïve to believe that these practices, whether unconscious, implicit, or deliberate, will not be a part of the Black experience. Although I will always be concerned about racism and discriminatory behaviors, this process must focus on my actions and behaviors. I did the right thing by filing a complaint against the project manager and the manager in my previous employment because their behaviors warranted those actions. But this does not take away the sadness I feel for my daughter, my grandson, and the generations of Black folk who will deal with hateful, aggressive, and disrespectful attitudes and behaviors from people who hate the color of their skin.

I can still feel the adrenaline I felt when these events occurred. The mind and body are connected and synchronized; retrieving memories can be emotionally and physically draining. Also, it is essential to note those feelings that may surface to garner a better perspective of the intensity of behaviors. I recognize my behavior of staying silent or allowing issues to fester and then boil over is problematic for my aspirational self. I continue implementing practices to counter unwanted behaviors to turn them into behaviors that aid in reaching my future goals for myself.

Every journaling session gives me further insight and wisdom about myself. Experiential learning is a necessary construct that strengthens this leadership framework. Reflection establishes knowledge when there is acknowledgment and transformation of the experience. The journaling process is to acknowledge history and respect that memories are rehearsals. Memories are a means for us to practice for the future, so reflection is not just for remembrance and a means to transfer experiences; it is to transform ourselves to manifest our visions for the future and our future selves.

Journal Exercise 2

For this journal entry, spend some time thinking about some of your behaviors. Be as detailed as possible about the origins of these behaviors. Give yourself grace as you go through this process. Be honest with your recollection and try to understand the anchoring of your behaviors which can unlock essential details about your identity. What triggers these behaviors and some of the outcomes? Then determine whether these behaviors should become habits or whether the behavior should be modified or changed to align with your self-perceptions and self-conceptions of your identity.

Memory Entries: Behaviors

Behavior Reflection Takeaways:

My Habit Reflection

One habit I recognized that I wanted to work on is interjecting my thoughts before the person I am speaking with finishes their thoughts. In layman's terms, I "cut people off when they talk." I realized that being a good listener is an essential leadership quality on my identity journey. Understanding that, I identified my habit of not listening when people talked because I was eager to respond. When I decided to be a better listener, I took the time to understand how I developed that habit.

After pages and pages of journaling and recollection, I pinpointed where this habit formed. When my parents passed in 2018, I had an opportunity to spend quality time with my siblings. I am the seventh of nine children and the first girl born after five boys. My twin brother and sister are two years younger than me. Growing up, my family would entertain ourselves by having debates. We would debate current sports, politics, music, or pop culture topics. When we reminisced on this time as we grieved the loss of our parents, my younger sister and I remembered how we felt when we could not get a word in because my brothers would monopolize the conversations.

I recalled how we would jump in and interject to express our thoughts. In this memory, this is where the habit of not allowing people to finish their thoughts started or at least intensified. This reflection has helped me to consciously work on this unwanted habit when I am in conversations. This habit has not stopped, but I have begun eliminating it from my identity schema.

Habits may be more challenging to recognize. Daily routines such as brushing teeth, going to work, and eating dinner differ from what this exercise tries to identify. When examining leadership schemas, the habits affecting your decision-making and building and maintaining relationships are essential to acknowledge and understand. More time spent on behavioral reflection may help in pinpointing habits.

Be gentle with yourself when recognizing your habits, especially the undesirable ones. These things do not make you an inadequate or ineffective leader. Still, they can help you become a better person and a more efficient leader.

Remember: Each time you reflect and journal, try to go deeper and tackle a different level of the mind: conscious, preconscious, and unconscious.

Journal Exercise 3

For this journal entry, spend some time thinking about some of your habits. Be as detailed as possible about the origins of these habits. Give yourself grace as you go through this process. Be honest with your recollection and try to understand the anchoring of your habits which can unlock essential details about your identity. What triggers these habits and some of the outcomes? Then determine whether these habits should be modified or changed to align with your self-perceptions and self-conceptions of your identity.

Memory Entries: Habits

Habit Reflection Takeaways:

The Assignment – Habits and Behaviors

Now acknowledge the behaviors and habits you exhibit. It's time to understand their roots and discern whether these actions and attitudes will help you manifest your aspirational leadership schema. Pay close attention to those habits and behaviors you believe do not serve your identity goals. Examine the WHO, WHAT, WHEN, WHERE, WHY, and HOW of these habits and behaviors to give you the knowledge you need to transform

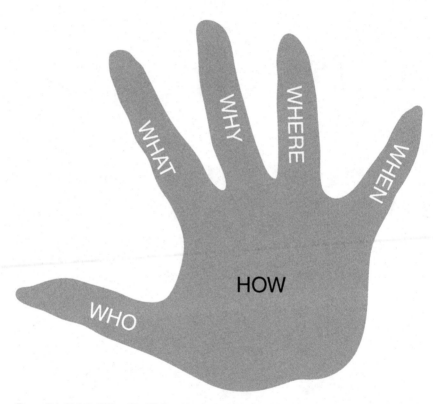

Figure 7.1 SLIM's "Give Me 5" Details about Habit and Behavior Foundation

When was the habit formed,
Where was the habit formed,
How was that habit formed,
Who or *What* may have encouraged that habit,
Why do you believe this habit has been sustained?

Habits and behaviors you want to explore:

1Habit or Behavior_____
Memory Entries: *When* was this habit formed?

Memory Entries: *Where* was this habit formed?

Memory Entries: *How* was this habit formed?

Memory Entries: *Who or What* may have encouraged this habit?

Memory Entries: *Why* do you believe this habit has been sustained?

2 Habit or Behavior_____

Memory Entries: *When* was this habit formed?

Memory Entries: *Where* was this habit formed?

Memory Entries: *When* was this habit formed?

Memory Entries: *Who or What* may have encouraged this habit?

Memory Entries: *Why* do you believe this habit has been sustained?

The Assignment – Strengths and Weaknesses

In this assignment, identify behaviors and habits you may need clarification on adding to your leadership identity schema. List the strengths and weaknesses of these behaviors and habits, determine whether the drawbacks outweigh the strengths or vice-versa, and if they should be included as part of your schematic model. Remember, the goal is growth and transformation, so even if the behavior or habit aligns with your leadership identity, reflect on how it can be stronger and more reliable to manifest your idealized self.

Schematic Model

Once you have identified these habits, begin to take note of those that have the potential to remain a part of your schematic framework according to the ledger below. Modifications of this schematic model will happen throughout the SLIM evolutionary process. Remember, you will go through the journaling process many times, so take your time to align your model with any behavior or habit at this stage. Determining what habits and behaviors align with your idealized leadership identity is essential. Later chapters present this model, where developing your schematic leadership model will provide your identity blueprint.

Table 7.1 Example: Behavior and Habits Strengths and Weaknesses

Weaknesses	Potential Strengths	How it is applied to individualized schematic model (SLIM)
Interrupting people while they speak	Change the eagerness to speak into an eagerness to listen. Shift the goal of the conversation.	Creates a habit of becoming a good listener that strengthens leadership abilities including knowledge that can help decisions.

Table 7.2 Behavior and Habits Strengths and Weaknesses – Assignment

Weaknesses	*Potential Strengths*	*How it is applied to individualized schematic model (SLIM)*

SCHEMATIC MODEL

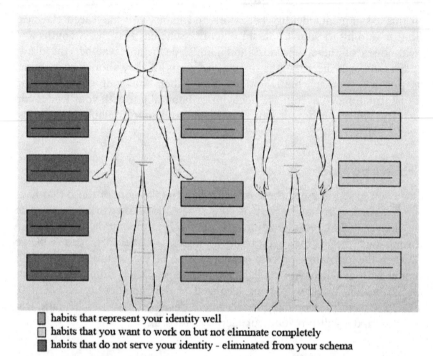

☐ habits that represent your identity well
☐ habits that you want to work on but not eliminate completely
☐ habits that do not serve your identity - eliminated from your schema

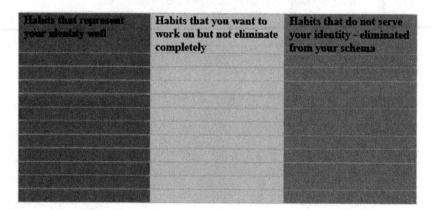

Habits that represent your identity well	Habits that you want to work on but not eliminate completely	Habits that do not serve your identity - eliminated from your schema

Figure 7.2 SLIM's Leadership Identity Schematic Model

Notes

1 Linking habits to identity may sustain newly formed behaviors and may thus lead to more effective behavior change interventions.

Verplanken, B., & Sui, J. (2019). Habit and Identity: Behavioral, Cognitive, Affective, and Motivational Facets of an Integrated Self. *Frontiers in Psychology, 10.* https://doi.org/10.3389/fpsyg.2019.01504

Ajzen, I., & Fishbein, M. (1975). A Bayesian Analysis of Attribution Processes. *Psychological Bulletin, 82*(2), 261

Deci, E. L., & Ryan, R. M. (1991). A Motivational Approach to Self: Integration in Personality. *Nebraska Symposium on Motivation,* 38, 237–288.

Rise, J., Sheeran, P., & Hukkelberg, S. (2010). The Role of Self-identity in the Theory of Planned Behavior: A Meta-analysis. *Journal of Applied Social Psychology, 40*(5), 1085–1105.

2   Rise, J., Sheeran, P., & Hukkelberg, S. (2010). The Role of Self-identity in the Theory of Planned Behavior: A Meta-analysis. *Journal of Applied Social Psychology, 40*(5), 1085–1105.

3   Galla, B. M., & Duckworth, A. L. (2015). More than Resisting Temptation: Beneficial Habits Mediate the Relationship between Self-control and Positive Life Outcomes. *Journal of Personality and Social Psychology, 109*(3), 508.

4   Wood, W., & Rünger, D. (2016). Psychology of Habit. *Annual Review of Psychology, 67,* 289–314

5   Blasi A. (1984). Moral Identity: Its Role in Moral Functioning. In Kurtines W., Gewirtz J. (Eds.), *Morality, Moral Behavior and Moral Development* (pp. 128–139). New York: Wiley.

6   Wagner, N. F., & Northoff, G. (2014). Habits: Bridging the Gap between Personhood and Personal Identity. *Frontiers in Human Neuroscience, 8,* 330.

7   Sheldon, K. M., & Elliot, A. J. (1999). Goal Striving, Need Satisfaction, and Longitudinal Well-Being: The Self-Concordance Model. *Journal of Personality and Social Psychology, 76*(3), 482.

Aarts, H., & Dijksterhuis, A. (2000). Habits as Knowledge Structures: Automaticity in Goal-directed Behavior. *Journal of Personality and Social Psychology, 78*(1), 53.

Verplanken, B., & Holland, R. W. (2002). Motivated Decision Making: Effects of Activation and Self-Centrality of Values on Choices and Behavior. *Journal of Personality and Social Psychology, 82*(3), 434.

Bardi, A., & Schwartz, S. H. (2003). Values and Behavior: Strength and Structure of Relations. *Personality and Social Psychology Bulletin, 29*(10), 1207–1220.

Hitlin, S. (2003). Values as the Core of Personal Identity: Drawing Links between Two Theories of Self. *Social Psychology Quarterly,* 118–137

Gatersleben, B., Murtagh, N., & Abrahamse, W. (2014). Values, Identity, and Pro-environmental Behaviour. *Contemporary Social Science, 9*(4), 374–392.

8   Gardner, B., & Lally, P. (2018). Modeling Habit Formation and its Determinants. *The Psychology of Habit,* 207–229.

9   Kolb, D. A., Boyatzis, R. E., & Mainemelis, C. (2014). Experiential Learning Theory: Previous Research and New Directions. *Perspectives on Thinking, Learning, and Cognitive Styles,* 227–248. doi: 10.4324/9781410605986-9

10 Kolb, D. A. (1987). Experiential Learning: Experience as the Source of Learning and Development. *Journal of Organizational Behavior, 8*(4), 359–360. doi:10.1002/job.4030080408

Chapter 8

Phase IV, Part 3

The Work – Self-Trust

What in the world does <u>trust</u> have to do with <u>identity</u>?
What is trust?
Trust is a firm belief in the reliability, truth, ability, or strength of someone or something.

For centuries trust has been the subject of many psychological and philosophical studies. One significant indicator of trust is being trustworthy. Sometimes refraining from providing information and feelings displays a lack of trust. In turn, these behaviors and actions cause a mutual sense of distrust. Accountability, competence, concern for others, integrity, and shared values are necessary for a mutually trusting relationship because trust is not a one-way street. The construct about trust often lost is that trust needs to be commanded and received upon demand. Our dependable behaviors, delivering on time, keeping our word, and investing time in building relationships help establish trust. Trust can also indicate self-efficacy and how you feel about yourself. Many distrusting people are themselves not trustworthy. The journey of identity helps to unravel factors and experiences that are key to unlocking attitudes, behaviors, and habits that block your ability to be vulnerable enough to be trustworthy and to trust others, but more importantly, trust yourself.[1]

According to *Harvard Business Review*, trust is essential to developing individual relationships. Leaders who cannot inspire trust cannot lead; there will be no followership.[2] In his book *The Trusted Advisor*, Charles M. Green noted the importance of self-orientation in the definition of trust. "Lowering self-orientation" can improve trustworthiness, says Green. "Practice limiting your talking with others to 60–120 seconds," "Practice thinking out loud," and "Don't think less of yourself–just think of yourself less."[3] SLIM focuses on self-orientation and does not initially seek to analyze and examine the team or the organizational trust dynamics. Concentrating on the trustworthiness of self allows us to explore our behaviors and how our lack of trust in ourselves hinders our trustworthiness with others. Self-trust is not that you will have solutions to all your

DOI: 10.4324/9781003394051-8

problems or always do the right things. Trusting yourself is knowing that you have a foundation of values and integrity on which you operate. A person who trusts themselves has clarity in how and why they make their decisions. These characteristics are not to be mistaken for being over-confident or egotistical. One must thoroughly understand oneself to discern when and how to lower self-orientation. This knowledge comes from spending the time to know how you feel about yourself and finding safety in that to extend trust to others. The question to answer at the beginning of this self-discovery journey is: DO YOU TRUST YOURSELF?

Self-Trust and the Past

As leaders go through this evolutionary process of discovery and evaluation of their history to strengthen their leadership identity, it is essential to emphasize a few things about past experiences and trust.

Many people wish they could go back and change their decisions and behaviors. As human beings, we should embrace every feeling and emotion that comes our way. But, when a person is consumed with those emotions regarding outcomes they cannot change, it becomes a problem. The mindset of regret is a barrier to self-trust. When something terrible happens, it is human nature to wish it had not occurred. Even taking a moment to ponder and learn from the experience is not harmful to how we feel about ourselves. Regret and shame can hinder how we trust ourselves. Process the event and take what will heal and strengthen you for the future.

Worry is another catalyst for becoming untrustworthy of self. Whether it is worrying about the past or future, this emotion represents a lack of trust in the work that you put in and the planning that you are conducting for what is to come. Self-trust requires balancing emotions, feelings, and actions. Building the leadership identity schema will frame boundaries that leaders can use to help stabilize emotions and behaviors.

Self-trust helps establish confidence, and this confidence will make decision-making more manageable and can help leaders develop social capital with their team. Confidence is infectious, and when leaders show up confidently and can trust in their own decisions, their team is likely to follow and take their lead.

Trust is a practice so let's begin (or continue) doing the work!

The Assignment – Do You Trust Yourself?

Take some time to do a self-inventory of the following to discern your trust and trustworthiness in yourself. Write about thoughts, experiences, behaviors, or habits that support how you deliver on these essential trust-worthy factors.

ACCOUNTABILITY

How are you accountable to yourself?

CREDIBILITY

Do you do what you say you are going to do for yourself? Do you make plans for yourself only to back out?

COMPETENCE

Do you have the necessary skills to meet your goals and expectations of yourself? If not, what are your plans to acquire that knowledge and skills?

CONCERN FOR SELF

Do you take time out for self-care? Do you put others' interests before your own? How do you show up for yourself?

INTEGRITY

Are you honest with yourself? Do you adhere to your morals, principles, and values? If not, in what instances and why?

SHARED VALUES

Are your values a derivative of your family's or friends' values? Do they align with your aspirational self? Identify those values that align with others but no longer serve you.

Notes

1 Stoner, J. L. (2018, January 16). The 5 Levels of Trust. Seapoint Center for Collaborative Leadership. Retrieved May 15, 2022, from https://seapointcenter. com/the-levels-of-trust/
2 Baldwin, J. (2020, August 27). How Trustworthy Are You? *Harvard Business Review*. https://hbr.org/2008/05/how-trustworthy-are-you
3 Maister, D., Green, C. H., & Galford, R. (2021). *The Trusted Advisor*. Simon & Schuster.

Chapter 9

Phase IV, Part 4
The Work – Removing the Shade

How to remove the Blinders that block you from being your authentic self

All the exercises and journal entries in this workbook help to remove or re-evaluate behaviors, attitudes, habits, and practices that may prevent leaders from becoming who they want to be. Eliminating things that hinder you from reaching your ideal self is an essential component of SLIM that allows attributes you assign to your identity to shine through by providing a process that supports the evolution of self-discovery.

The Assignment – Removing the Shade

What is the SHADE process?

Figure 9.1 Removing the SHADE in search of your identity

DOI: 10.4324/9781003394051-9

The Evolution

Removing the S*H*A*D*E in search of
IDENTITY

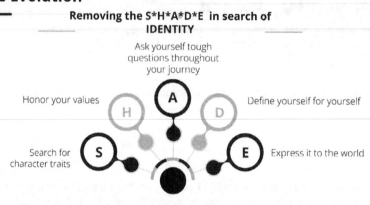

Figure 9.2 The Evolutionary Process of Removing the SHADE

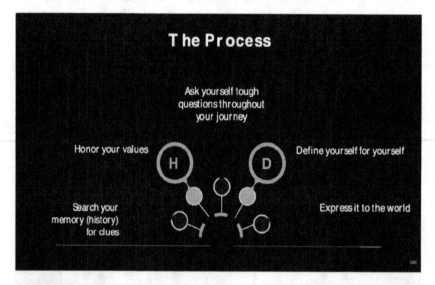

Figure 9.3 The SHADE Process

S – Search your memory (history) for clues

   With every major change in your life, revisit your list and update it.

H – Honor your values

   Identify family and cultural values that you believe in.

A – Ask the tough questions

   Continue to ask yourself tough questions about your behavior, values, and attitudes.

D – Define yourself for yourself
Know your framework and your foundation. Understand how you have designed and framed your "house", which is your identity. Examine your attic and "Go into the basement!"

E – Express it to the world!
Move in the house you constructed (your schema).
Dwell in your entire house – Live out loud WHO YOU ARE!

Remove Filters & Explore The SHADE!

As you journal, revisit SHADE

S. Search for character traits. **With every major change in your life, revisit your list and update it!**
Periodically update your list as you experience life changes

H. Honor your Values. **Identify family and cultural values that you believe in!**
It's important to identify those values and morals that you feel deeply about and practice daily.

A. Ask the tough questions! **And continue to ask tough questions!**
Ask the tough questions about yourself - the decisions you make and the actions you take. Are they that in line with your values and character? If not, why? Is it from an honest place?

D. Define yourself for yourself. **Know your Framework and Foundation?**
Without this you are moving blindly! It begins with your character, values and morals

E. Express it to the World! **Move in WHO YOU ARE!**
Know that understanding who you are is a process! Remember it's Chess not Checkers! It takes time, practice, strategic thought, patience, endurance, honesty, creative thinking, and problem solving skills!

Figure 9.4 Summary of SHADE

S – SEARCH YOUR MEMORY (HISTORY) FOR CLUES

Document clues about your identity. With every major change in your life, revisit your list and update it!

H – HONOR YOUR VALUES

Identify family and cultural values that you believe in!

It is important to identify those values and morals that you feel deeply about and practice daily.

A – ASK THE TOUGH QUESTIONS
And continue to ask tough questions!

Ask the tough questions about yourself – the decisions you make and the actions you take.

Are they in line with your values and character? If not, why? Is it from an honest place?

Advancing knowledge of behavior/habits:	Strengthening your self-identity:
• *How has this behavior/habit changed how you see yourself? Has the behavior/habit progressed or shiftedf over time? How? Why?* • *What new behaviors/habits have resulted?* • *What, if any, is the impact on how you make decisions? On ypur values? on how you see others?*	• *What do you think about yourself?* • *What is your perception of your leadership identity?* • *What are the behaviors/habits, attitudes, and values of your idealized self?* • *What changes do you need to make to manifest your idealized self?*
Building social capital and social networks • *How has this behavior impacted your team? Or colleagues? community?* • *How are social norms shifting from your change i n behavior, if at all?* • *To what extent has this behavior change stregthened your relationships?*	**Increasing Your Trustworthiness** • *Are you accountable for your behaviors/habits? if so, how? if not, why?* • *Are you credible (do people believe you and believe in what you say?) are you reliable? (Can what you do and say be trusted based on evidence?* • *Are you competent in your work? Do you share values with your professional and social netwroks?*

Figure 9.5 Example questions to ponder when examining SHADE

D – DEFINE YOURSELF FOR YOURSELF
Know your Framework and Foundation.

Without this, you are moving blindly! It begins with your character, values, and morals – what are they?

E – EXPRESS IT TO THE WORLD!
Move-in WHO YOU ARE!

Know that understanding who you are is a process. Remember, it's chess, not checkers. It takes time, practice, strategic thought, patience, endurance, honesty, creative thinking, and problem-solving skills. Redefining yourself is necessary as you experience life. As your environment changes so do you. When the people around you change, how does that affect you? As long as you take control over your identity and define it for yourself, it will be difficult for you to subscribe to who others say you are if it does not align with your framing.

WRITE IT DOWN – WHO ARE YOU?

Chapter 10

Phase V
The Build – Schematic Leadership Identity Model

It's time to build your schematic blueprint!

Below is an example of my behavioral and habit identifications taken from my journaling experience shared in Chapter 2. Revisit your journaling entries and the assignments to pull out those habits and behaviors to include in your schematic leadership model. It is okay if you need clarification on the relevancy of a habit or behavior to your leadership schema. Document it here, as you will have many opportunities to modify this list as you analyze the constructs deeper with each journaling exercise.

The Assignment – Schematic Blueprint

How to connect habits and behaviors to your values? Build your leadership schema from your journaling reflection and the assignments.

Below, build your leadership identity schema by documenting some key findings from your journaling and exercises completed in earlier chapters. The first few times through, it is okay to include all the behaviors, habits, and values revealed during the process. Identify all the traits in this list;

Figure 10.1 Leadership Identity Schema

DOI: 10.4324/9781003394051-10

BEHAVIORS (RESPONSES)	HABITS	VALUES
Being alone	Order	Loyality and a sense of belonging
Stubbornness	Cleanliness	My mother's love and frienship
Intolerance for racism, disrespect,		Empathetic and open to others
discriminatory behaviors, attitudes, etc.		Community
Cautions of establishing new relationships		Do not like ulitmatums, being pressured
Quick to make decisions		
Internalize feelings		

Figure 10.2 Behaviors, Habits, and Values Example

later, during the process, you can remove those things that do not serve the leader you wish to become.

As you process your self-discovery journey, build, modify, and reflect on your Schematic Leadership Identity Model below. Leaders should revisit the journal entries and assignments. Note behaviors and habits that align with the current leadership schema, those you are unsure of, and those that do not connect at this stage in your evolutionary journey. Write in pencil because these may shift or change as you reflect on and design your leadership identity.

BEHAVIORS (RESPONSES)	HABITS	VALUES

Figure 10.3 Behaviors, Habits, and Values Assignment

Chapter 11

Phase VI

The Anchor – Sustaining Schematic Leadership Changes

The Change Process

A change process can ensure accountability for the changes and modifications to your identity schema. This process will help you reach your leadership goals. The red and yellow behaviors and habits in your schematic leadership model, updated in Chapter 10, are focused elements for the change process. Change does not occur because of new technology, processes, or systems. Change happens because people decide to change and adapt to those changes. Change requires a commitment so that it is sustainable. Personal change is the most taxing change that a person can experience. In society, especially on social media, it is not acceptable to reveal any imperfections. Still, these blemishes make us unique and provide clues about reaching our aspirational selves. As leaders re-evaluate their leadership identity, some may find it challenging to acknowledge cracks in their leadership schema. Acknowledgment and a willingness to change are essential, but there needs to be a means to evaluate and measure these changes.

Social and environmental factors generate a transactional exchange, forming a blueprint for developing this leadership model. Learning styles can change depending on situations and circumstances. Change is the linchpin of this leadership model. Practicing experiential learning through reflection is vital to the pathway for change and strengthening one's leadership identity in this proposed leadership framework.

The SLIM framework suggests an accountability partner who will ride alongside the leader as they journey down the path to re-assess, redesign, and rebuild their leadership identity. An accountability partner does not need to know the details of the SLIM process to be a support on the volutionary journey. This support system ensures the manifestation of the leader's desired changes. This partnership should be a unique construction between the leaders and someone they trust and feel comfortable sharing information with and who can help discern changes in their behaviors and attitudes.

DOI: 10.4324/9781003394051-11

Change Behavior or Habit example:

	Step	Strategies to Drive Change
Habit or Behavior: *Interrupting people when they speak*		
1	Barriers	This habit hinders successful communication which hinders moving into the next role or prevents relationships from growing. I will continue to do the work to understand my need to interject and the source of how it started.
2	Support System	Ask a colleague to inform me when it happens in their presence. Ask my family to stop me if this habit manifests while speaking with them. I will communicate this vision to trusted colleagues, family, and friends.
3	Forward Thinking	I see myself understanding people more because I am taking a pause and really listening to them. My team will be strengthened, and my leadership capital will be increased.
4	Establish small wins	Limit interruptions in conversations a few times a day, even with family and friends.
5	Ultimate goal and timeframe	Seek to eliminate the habit in every conversation. Document progress and work to eliminate this habit in 12 months.
6	Anchor the Changes in Personal and Corporate Cultures	Conduct team building exercises that require listening – pausing – breathing. Continue to understand that being first or fast does not always equate to being the best or most effective.

Figure 11.1 Change Behavior or Habit Example

The change model questionnaire deals with the personal changes that may occur in leaders who may be hesitant or unwilling to change their approach to leadership and decision-making. Identifying and documenting practices needed for progress can help leaders adapt and transform their leadership identity accordingly.

Identify each habit and behavior from the schematic leadership model. Address the strategies that will drive the change needed to meet the schematic leadership identity model presented in Chapter 10. Feel free to add actions to help you manifest and sustain the required change.

Utilize the tables below to highlight essential notes regarding habits and behaviors that may help the change process.

Brief description of the behavior or habit	History/Memory/Experience List the origins of the behavior/action/decision. Was it passed down through your bloodline? Learned behavior through social netwroks? Something you recalled in your oast.

Figure 11.2 Change Behavior or Habit Assignment

Behavior or Habit	Self-Reflective Notes

Figure 11.3 Behavior or Habit Self-Reflective Notes

Change Behavior or Habit:

Habit or Behavior:	
Actions	Strategies to Drive Change
1 Identify Barriers	
2 Identify Support System	
3 Forward Thinking	
4 Establish small wins	
5 Ultimate goals and timeframe	
6 Describe necessary changes in personal and corporate cultures	

Figure 11.4 Behavior or Habit Origins

Chapter 12

Phase VII
The Remodel – Begin Again

Now that you have gone through the journaling process and assignments that identified behaviors and habits that may or may not align with your leadership schema, re-evaluating your leadership identity is complete, right? The answer is no. This chapter does not denote the end of the leadership identity process. Self-improvement is never-ending. It's a systematic process, so consider this a new beginning!

Your identity *evolution* is the recognition of the continuous changes in your leadership identity journey as you grow and experience life. Modifications, updates, and deletions will be consistent as long as you continue to live life and encounter new environments, people, and situations. SLIM is a system, so continue to review and practice the series of assignments and journal entries to strengthen your understanding of your history, which informs your behavior, habits, and values. The evolution process is like an onion. Each cycle through the work in this phase, layers are peeled back to unveil the undercurrents of how you think, learn, and process memory, which results in how you make decisions. The evolution journey helps further discern how habits contribute to behaviors contrary to the person's aspirational and desired identity outcomes. Inputs and outputs can be instrumental in identifying and rectifying unconscious and implicit biases that result in problematic decisions and can hinder how you build and sustain relationships.

The design of the evolutionary phase is to take a pause. This phase potentially unravels deeply embedded memories and information that reveal pertinent details regarding one's leadership identity. What does it mean? How does it benefit the path that you are on professionally and personally? Do the outcomes give you clarity, or are you asking yourself more questions? How can you "Take yourself off the shelf?" Have you "Removed the Shade" from your identity?

SLIM is a system rooted in Todorov's Theory of the Narrative. Our lives are stories worth telling. But we must write them ourselves – the beginning (equilibrium), the conflict/climax (disequilibrium), the point of view (acknowledgment), the resolution (solving), and as we have learned

DOI: 10.4324/9781003394051-12

throughout this book, the evolution, or the beginning again (equilibrium),[1] because every day we live has the potential for new challenges, successes, and experiences.

REMEMBER:

Your identity **REVOLUTION** will not be televised because it's an

EVOLUTIONARY

process of self-reflective work!

Let's continue to evolve and be our best selves, culminating in our leadership identities.

Note

1 Todorov, T., & Weinstein, A. (1969). Structural Analysis of Narrative. *NOVEL: A Forum on Fiction, 3*(1), 70. https://doi.org/10.2307/1345003

Index

Printed in the United States
by Baker & Taylor Publisher Services